TOTAL ECLIPSE

TOTAL ECLIPSE

Christopher Hampton

Faber and Faber
BOSTON · LONDON

AUTHOR'S NOTE

As is often the case, the text printed here differs in several respects from the finished released film. Time and budget considerations, as well as the usual director's prerogatives as to the length and shape of the piece, have brought about a number of modifications. To take an obvious example, my organization of the script into eight sections titled according to and roughly corresponding in length to the eight sections of Rimbaud's *Une Saison en Enfer* was of great help to me in structuring the script, but could not easily be applied to the different emphases of the finished film, which was able to devote much less time to the African Rimbaud than the script suggested.

Publishing the script in this form, however, should not be taken to imply any criticism of Agnieszka Holland's lucid, forthright and powerful film, which I'm happy to endorse here: it was simply that, at the publisher's suggestion, I agreed that the fuller version here presented might be of interest to readers.

C.H.

Total Eclipse had its first public showing in the United States on November 1, 1995. It opened theatrically on November 3, 1995.

The cast includes:

ARTHUR RIMBAUD	Leonardo DiCaprio
PAUL VERLAINE	David Thewlis
MATHILDE VERLAINE	Romane Bohringer
ISABELLE RIMBAUD	Dominique Blanc

Music	Jan A. P. Kaczmarek
Director of Photography	Yorgos Arvanitis, A.F.C.
Editor	Isabel Lorente
Production Designer	Dan Weil
Costume Designer	Pierre-Yves Gayraud
Co-producers	Philip Hinchcliffe and Cat Villiers
Executive Producers	Jean-Yves Asselin, Staffan Ahrenberg, Pascale Faubert
Produced by	Jean-Pierre Ramsay Levi
Directed by	Agnieszka Holland

A Fit Production / Portman Production / SFP Cinema /
K2 Co-production
A Fine Line Features release

EXT. RAILWAY STATION DAWN

It's September 1871. The platform at Charleville railway station in the Ardennes is more or less deserted, but the CAMERA *soon discovers and begins to examine an extremely striking sixteen-year-old boy. He has large, reddish hands, none too clean. His grey eyes are piercing, their expression merciless. His tie hangs loose round his neck like a piece of old string. His suit is frayed and shabby, the sleeves too short and the trousers ending an inch above his blue socks. His black boots are caked with mud. He's bareheaded. This is* ARTHUR RIMBAUD.

A caption:

I   MAUVAIS SANG

Presently, we hear the VOICE *of* PAUL VERLAINE, *quiet, reflective.*

VERLAINE (V.O.)
Sometimes he speaks, in a kind of tender dialect, of the death which causes repentance, of the unhappy men who certainly exist, of painful tasks and heartrending departures.

A train is puffing slowly into the station. RIMBAUD *moves forward towards the edge of the platform.*

INT. TRAIN COMPARTMENT DAY

RIMBAUD *sits in a corner of the compartment by the window puffing on an old clay pipe, much to the displeasure of his* FELLOW PASSENGERS— *a* MIDDLE-AGED WOMAN, *sitting opposite him, and an* ELDERLY COUPLE *in the two other corners of the compartment. Outside, the autumnal landscape.*

VERLAINE (V.O.)
In the hovels where we got drunk, he wept, looking at those who surrounded us, the cattle of poverty.

EXT. VIADUCT DAY

The train waits, stalled on a high viaduct, sharply outlined against the sky.

VERLAINE (V.O.)

He lifted up drunks in the black streets. He had the pity a bad
mother has for small children.

INT./EXT. COMPARTMENT DAY

RIMBAUD *looks out of the window, no longer smoking his pipe. After a
while, he rises to his feet, and to the alarm of his* FELLOW PASSENGERS,
*opens the door of the compartment. Below, over the edge of the viaduct, a
vertiginous drop, which we contemplate from* RIMBAUD'S P.O.V.

VERLAINE (V.O.)

He moved with the grace of a little girl at catechism. He pre-
tended to know about everything, business, art, medicine.

EXT. VIADUCT DAY

RIMBAUD, *seen from below, framed in the open doorway of the compartment. Suddenly, he steps forward, arms outstretched, and flies, at a steep
angle, upwards and out of frame.*

4

> VERLAINE (V.O.)
> I followed him, I had to!

INT. VERLAINE'S LODGINGS DAWN 1892

VERLAINE *opens an eye. He's forty-eight now, but looks older, hollow-eyed, ravaged, his beard, moustache and bald head giving him the appearance of a satyr. He rubs a hand experimentally over his face.*

ANOTHER ANGLE *reveals more of the squalid attic room; and that* VERLAINE *is in bed with* EUGÉNIE KRANTZ, *also in her forties, fast asleep, her hair, dyed a garish red, splashed across the grey bolster.*

VERLAINE *reaches down and draws a cracked chamber-pot from under the bed. He frowns and utters a small groan as he notices that its contents are frozen. Then he glances at* EUGÉNIE, *sees she's still asleep and quietly slides the pot back under the bed.*

VERLAINE *pushes back the covers and gingerly steps out of bed. He's wearing a shirt over long grey darned combinations. He tiptoes across the room and reaches for* EUGÉNIE'S *handbag, lying on the table. He's hardly got it open, though, when* EUGÉNIE *is sitting up, glaring at him across the room.*

> EUGÉNIE
> Hands off.

VERLAINE *lets go of the handbag, his expression sheepish.*

> You want some money, you earn it. I do.

> VERLAINE
> I just thought maybe . . .

> EUGÉNIE
> And a lot more than you ever come home with.

> VERLAINE
> That's because you're so beautiful.

She isn't: she looks coarse and brassy; but sitting up in bed, naked, she's a somehow commanding figure. VERLAINE *moves across, back to the bed, but she intercepts his outstretched hand.*

EUGÉNIE

And none of that either. You take that poem you wrote last night, you go to Vanier and you sell it.

VERLAINE *turns back obediently and crosses to the cramped, chaotic table he uses for a desk. On top of the mass of books, magazines and papers is a sheet of paper on which is written, in a neat but shaky hand, a poem of three four-line stanzas, much amended, with many crossings-out and afterthoughts.* VERLAINE *reaches for it and contemplates it for a moment.*

VERLAINE

One more verse, I think. Just to complete the thought.

EUGÉNIE

If it's not there, they won't miss it, will they?

VERLAINE *hesitates; then puts the poem down again, yielding to her reasoning, his expression rueful.*

EXT. GARE DE L'EST DAY 1871

VERLAINE *is twenty-seven now, expensively and quite formally dressed, already going bald, but in other respects a total contrast to the derelict carnal hulk of the previous scene. He waits at the barrier with his friend* CHARLES CROS, *a couple of years older, a tall dandy with frizzy hair and a mournful moustache. The train has arrived and passengers are streaming past.* `

RIMBAUD *passes through the barrier, moving solitary through the crowd, looking around, coming towards* VERLAINE *and* CROS.

VERLAINE *notices him: he frowns for a moment, evidently struck by* RIMBAUD*'s appearance.* RIMBAUD, *for his part, glances at the fashionable pair and passes by.* VERLAINE *returns his attention to the oncoming crowd.*

EXT. STREET IN PARIS DAY

RIMBAUD *is walking, fast. This is to become one of our most characteristic images of him: restless, staring straight ahead, always driving himself onward. For once, however, he's distracted by something, breaks his stride.*

The street is one of those damaged in the recent civil war and destruction of the Commune. Buildings are mutilated, scorched and bullet-scarred, their windows blown out. In one place, a couple of houses have burned to the ground, leaving only a rubble-strewn, blackened gash in the continuity of the street. Rats scramble in the ruins. In front of this gap a knot of people surrounds a makeshift fire, next to which a couple of rats have been spitted, ready for roasting. A YOUNG MAN, *no older than* RIMBAUD, *breaks away from the group and extends a hand towards* RIMBAUD, *begging.*

RIMBAUD *stops. His hand goes to his pocket and he produces a few coins, probably all he has. He considers for a second, and then impulsively gives the* YOUNG MAN *all the coins. Then he strides on.*

INT. DRAWING-ROOM OF THE MAUTÉ DE FLEURVILLE
HOUSE EVENING

A handsome woman in her forties, VERLAINE*'s mother-in-law,* MME MAUTÉ DE FLEURVILLE, *sits at the piano, playing, with unquestionable ability, a transcription of the prelude to* Lohengrin. *Meanwhile, her daughter,* MATHILDE VERLAINE, *an attractive eighteen-year-old, eight months pregnant, arranges flowers in a cut-glass vase. It's a large room in a spacious house in Montmartre, discreetly affluent, furnished in the Louis-Philippe style.*

Once this is established, RIMBAUD *steps into the room. He's not seen by either of the women, so that when eventually he speaks, after standing silently in the doorway for a time, he startles them considerably.*

> RIMBAUD
Evening.

MME MAUTÉ *breaks off from her playing;* MATHILDE *stands, flower in hand, mouth open.*

I'm looking for Paul Verlaine.

> MME MAUTÉ
Are you . . . Monsieur Rimbaud?

RIMBAUD
Yes.

MME MAUTÉ
Monsieur Verlaine is not with you, then?

RIMBAUD
Well, no.

MATHILDE
He went to the station to meet you.

RIMBAUD
He doesn't know what I look like, does he?

By now MME MAUTÉ *is on her feet.*

MME MAUTÉ
I am Madame Mauté de Fleurville, Monsieur Verlaine's mother-in-law. And this is my daughter, Madame Verlaine.

RIMBAUD *exchanges perfunctory handshakes with the two women.*

MATHILDE
How did you get from the station?

RIMBAUD
Walked.

MME MAUTÉ
Perhaps you'd like a wash?

RIMBAUD
No.

MME MAUTÉ
Did you leave your luggage in the hall?

RIMBAUD
What?

MME MAUTÉ
Your luggage.

RIMBAUD
I have no luggage.

MME MAUTÉ

No luggage?

RIMBAUD

No.

MME MAUTÉ

Oh.

Silence. MME MAUTÉ *makes an effort to persevere.*

You're even younger than we imagined.

MATHILDE

How old are you?

MME MAUTÉ

Darling, it's not very polite to ask people their ages.

MATHILDE

I'm sorry, I was just so interested.

They both look at RIMBAUD, *but he seems disinclined to help them out. There's a longish silence, which eventually he breaks.*

RIMBAUD

I need a piss.

MME MAUTÉ *reacts as positively as she can, her smile queasy.*

INT. DINING-ROOM NIGHT

CLOSE *on* VERLAINE *as he stares, fascinated, across the table at* RIMBAUD. *There's silence at the moment; and when we eventually take* VERLAINE'S *P.O.V., we see that* RIMBAUD *is picking unenthusiastically at his food. Also at the table are* CLOS, MATHILDE *and* MME MAUTÉ.

VERLAINE

How old are you, if you don't mind my asking?

MATHILDE

He does.

RIMBAUD

Sixteen.

VERLAINE

Only you did say in your letter you were twenty-one.

RIMBAUD

Mm.

VERLAINE

I noticed you at the station, but I didn't think it could be you.

RIMBAUD

Likewise.

VERLAINE

Those poems you sent me were remarkable for someone of twenty-one. For someone of sixteen they're unprecedented.

RIMBAUD

That's why I told you I was twenty-one. I didn't want you to feel patronising before you'd read them.

VERLAINE

Of course, it all makes sense now. The fact your mother kept you at home with no money. You have left school?

RIMBAUD

Yes.

VERLAINE

I hope your mother isn't too angry with me.

RIMBAUD

No, once she found out you'd sent me the fare, she seemed quite happy.

MME MAUTÉ

You come from the Ardennes, don't you, Monsieur Rimbaud? Charleville?

RIMBAUD

Yes.

MME MAUTÉ

Pleasant town, Charleville, isn't it?

RIMBAUD
Last place on God's earth.

MATHILDE
What does your father do?

RIMBAUD
Drinks mostly, I believe. We haven't seen him for ten years.

MATHILDE
I'm sorry.

RIMBAUD
No need to be. He's very well out of it.

He pushes his plate away and produces from his pocket a repulsive old clay pipe and some matches. He lights the pipe, sucking noisily. MME MAUTÉ *watches him in some dismay.*

Mind if I smoke?

MME MAUTÉ
Not at all.

She makes a considerable effort and produces a friendly smile.

I was also very impressed with your poetry.

RIMBAUD *looks across at* VERLAINE, *frowning.*

RIMBAUD
You let her read it?

MME MAUTÉ
Perhaps you'd like to read something to us after dinner?

RIMBAUD
I don't think so.

MATHILDE
Oh, why not?

RIMBAUD
I don't want to. I never read out my poetry.

MATHILDE
All the other poets do. We have soirees. . . .

11

I'm not interested in what all the other poets do.

CROS
Don't you think poets can learn from one another?

RIMBAUD
Only if they're bad poets.

VERLAINE *can't resist a smile at the absolute confidence and truculence of this assertion.*

INT. ANDRÉ'S DAY

André's is a dingy café-bar, patronised by VERLAINE: *we shall see it over twenty years and more without it changing very much beyond a certain inevitable deterioration of the smoke-stained, low-ceilinged, poorly lit room.*

At the moment, however, what fills the SCREEN *is a glass of pure absinthe. A sugar-lump rests on the copper strainer across the top of the glass.* VERLAINE'*s hand picks up the jug of water and carefully begins to*

pour; the water passes through the strainer and begins to transform the liquid from dull brown to a swirling milky green.

> VERLAINE (V.O.)
> Do you know about this?

> RIMBAUD (V.O.)
> I know what it is.

> VERLAINE (V.O.)
> It's the poet's third eye. It melts glaciers.

A WIDER ANGLE: *he finishes pouring and pushes the drink across to* RIMBAUD. *Then he begins to dilute his own drink.* RIMBAUD *takes a sip and does his best not to reveal its powerful effect.* VERLAINE *considers him shrewdly for a moment.*

> VERLAINE
> Tell me, what do you think of my wife?

> RIMBAUD
> I don't know. What do you think of her?

> VERLAINE
> She's still only a child, of course.

RIMBAUD *takes another sip of absinthe and looks* VERLAINE *in the eye.*

> RIMBAUD
> So am I.

INT. MATHILDE'S BEDROOM NIGHT

MATHILDE *lies in her brass double bed next to* VERLAINE, *in his night-gown, who is reading from a sheaf of manuscript poems written in a clear, bold hand. What he's reading at the moment, in fact, is* Bateau Ivre.

> VERLAINE
> Listen to this: "Sometimes I've seen what people think they've seen."

> MATHILDE
> He's not how I imagined him.

13

VERLAINE *isn't listening to her: he finds something on another page.*

> VERLAINE
> "I've wept too many tears. Heartbreaking dawns,
> Each sun is gall, each moon is misery . . ."

> MATHILDE
> I prefer your poems. I don't really understand that kind of thing.

> VERLAINE
> No. No, this is something new.

INT. DRAWING-ROOM NIGHT

RIMBAUD, *holding a candlestick, his pipe clamped in his mouth, lets himself into the darkened room and crosses to inspect the bookshelves in* MAUTÉ's *library. He takes down a copy of* Les Fleurs du Mal *and then a copy of* Les Châtiments *by* Victor Hugo. *A glance at the flyleaf proves that this is a signed copy, inscribed with a dedication in Hugo's flowery hand. He continues to search, running his fingers along the spines of the fine leatherbound editions.*

INT. MATHILDE'S BEDROOM NIGHT

VERLAINE *is still reading: presently,* MATHILDE *gives a little gasp.*

> VERLAINE

What is it?

> MATHILDE

He's kicking.

VERLAINE *puts down the manuscript pages, draws back the covers, pulls up* MATHILDE*'s nightdress and puts his ear against the spot* MATHILDE *indicates on her swollen belly. For a moment, he listens, reacting delightedly as the baby kicks.* MATHILDE*'s expression, however, is thoughtful.*

Don't you think it would be more sensible to get one of your friends to put him up for a while?

VERLAINE*'s expression darkens. He takes his head away from her stomach and straightens up, frowning.*

> VERLAINE

People don't understand him. I'm the only one who understands him.

15

MATHILDE

Well, Daddy certainly won't understand him.

VERLAINE *sighs exasperatedly and speaks sharply to her.*

VERLAINE

You don't seem to realise, we had a revolution this year: which I supported. I could have been shot. If I hadn't been thrown out of my job, do you suppose I'd have accepted your father's damn charity for one instant?

MATHILDE *looks away, hurt.* VERLAINE *gathers up the manuscript and resumes reading, his expression righteously indignant.*

INT. DRAWING-ROOM NIGHT

RIMBAUD *has now accumulated a small pile of books; he looks around the room and his eye is taken by a handsome ivory crucifix on the wall. He looks at it for a moment, then reaches for it and puts it in his pocket. This done, he moves to the mantelpiece, on which is a row of china ornaments.*

He uses one of these to tap out his pipe, a purpose for which it's clearly not intended, and then picks up another, a very sentimentally conceived china dog, which he contemplates for a moment before dropping it into the grate so that it shatters. This seems to cheer him up, and for a second his features are enlivened by a grim smile.

INT. MATHILDE'S BEDROOM NIGHT

VERLAINE *looks up from the manuscript, clearly still annoyed, and glares briefly at* MATHILDE.

VERLAINE

For God's sake, all I'm doing is helping a friend. Why do we have to go through all this? I'm your husband.

MATHILDE, *uncertain, looks across at him unhappily. She reaches out to run her fingers through his hair.*

MATHILDE

I'm sorry, Paul.

VERLAINE

Are you trying to annoy me?

MATHILDE *takes her hand away, startled by his tone.*

MATHILDE

No.

VERLAINE

Well, don't.

INT. DRAWING-ROOM DAY

RIMBAUD *sits reading, slumped deep in an armchair with his boots resting on an occasional table. He looks up as the door opens to admit* M. MAUTÉ DE FLEURVILLE, *sixty-four, an imposing figure with a white beard.* MAUTÉ *doesn't immediately notice* RIMBAUD *and is therefore momentarily startled when the latter speaks, his tone hospitable.*

RIMBAUD

Morning. Everyone's out, I'm afraid. Or perhaps you've come to see the old boy?

MAUTÉ

The old boy?

RIMBAUD

Mauté de Fleurville. Not a friend of his, are you?

MAUTÉ

No.

RIMBAUD

No, I didn't think you were. As far as I can tell, he doesn't have any friends.

MAUTÉ

Really?

RIMBAUD

Apparently he defeats all comers with an unimpregnable combination of tediousness and avarice. I'm told he can't resist rifling the pockets of those who fall stunned by the monotony of his anecdotes.

17

He's on his feet now, circling MAUTÉ, *who's beginning to utter one or two indeterminate sounds, as his fury rises. But now* RIMBAUD *changes tack, producing the crucifix from his pocket.*

You wouldn't like to buy a crucifix, by any chance? I can let you have this on extremely reasonable terms. It's ivory, I think.

MAUTÉ

Who the hell are you?

RIMBAUD

I might ask you the same question. Except I'd be more polite.

MAUTÉ

I am Mauté de Fleurville.

RIMBAUD

Ah.

He's by the fireplace now; he indicates the shattered remains of the china dog.

I'm afraid I broke your dog last night.

MAUTÉ

Why?

RIMBAUD

Dogs are all liberals.

He leaves the room smartly: MAUTÉ, *entirely bewildered, remains rooted to the spot.*

EXT. MAUTÉ DE FLEURVILLE HOUSE RUE NICOLET DAY

RIMBAUD *leaves the substantial, three-storey house (no. 14), closes the front door firmly behind him, sets off briskly down the front path and out through the gate.*

He turns into the steep, narrow Montmartre street. It's raining lightly, but he seems indifferent, his expression absolutely serene and happy.

MAUTÉ *bursts into the room without knocking, shaking with rage.*
VERLAINE *and* MATHILDE, *still in bed, sit up, shocked by this invasion.*

> MAUTÉ
>
> Since when have you had the right to invite people to stay in
> this house without my permission?

> VERLAINE
>
> Since you offered to let us live here, I've treated it as our home.

> MAUTÉ
>
> So it is, your home, not a guest house.

> VERLAINE
>
> If I can't put up a guest in my home when I feel like it, I might
> as well live somewhere else.

> MAUTÉ
>
> If you weren't so idle, you might be able to afford to.

> VERLAINE
>
> You know very well, since the Commune . . .

> MAUTÉ
>
> Any excuse.

> VERLAINE
>
> I don't notice you working your fingers to the bone.

MAUTÉ *draws himself up, deciding to rise above this. When he speaks
again, his tone is icy.* MATHILDE *watches, her expression fearful.*

> MAUTÉ
>
> When you next see that hooligan, you'll kindly ask him to
> return the objects he's pilfered.

> VERLAINE
>
> What are you talking about?

> MAUTÉ
>
> He'll know what I mean.

> VERLAINE
>
> Then ask him yourself.

19

                              MAUTÉ
I'm happy to say he's left the house.

                              VERLAINE
What?

He jumps out of bed, at last genuinely concerned.

EXT. MONTMARTRE STREET DAY

VERLAINE *runs down the same steep Montmartre street, struggling with his umbrella.*

EXT. MAIN STREET DAY

VERLAINE *moves through the crowd, anxiously inspecting the passers-by.*

INT. ANDRÉ'S DAY

VERLAINE *moves around the dingy café, peering into dark corners, scrutinising every table.*

EXT. PARK EVENING

RIMBAUD *sits on a bench, his collar turned up against the still-falling rain, his expression dreamy. He reaches into a side-pocket, produces a carrot and begins to gnaw at it. Then, from another pocket, he produces the presentation copy of* Les Châtiments *and begins to read.*

Suddenly, VERLAINE *is standing above him.*

                              VERLAINE
Thank God, I thought I was never going to find you.

                              RIMBAUD
I'm all right.

                              VERLAINE
I don't know what that old bastard thought he was doing.

                              RIMBAUD
It's his house.

                              20

VERLAINE *reaches down to take* RIMBAUD*'s arm.*

> VERLAINE
>
> Come. We'll find you somewhere.

INT. ATTIC ROOM IN THE RUE DE BUCI EVENING

RIMBAUD *follows* VERLAINE *into a small attic room, crazily angled with a dormer window and a skylight, dusty and cobwebbed. There's a table with jug and basin and a mattress with some coverings on the floor.*

> VERLAINE
>
> It's not much, I'm afraid.

> RIMBAUD
>
> It's fine.

> VERLAINE
>
> Just for a few days.

EXT. STREETS NIGHT

A fiacre climbs towards Montmartre. VERLAINE*'s face at the window.*

INT. RIMBAUD'S ROOM NIGHT

RIMBAUD *slips off his jacket and starts to pluck at his shirt. It's as if he's just become aware that he's soaking wet. He starts to unbutton his shirt.*

EXT. RUE DE BUCI NIGHT

There's a small group of people gathered in the street, all looking up. Passers-by join the group, until a small crowd forms.

What they're looking at is RIMBAUD, *far above, standing on the windowsill of his room, backlit by candles. He's naked.*

INT. RIMBAUD'S ROOM NIGHT

RIMBAUD *leans over, picks up the bundle he's made of his clothes and drops them.*

EXT. RUE DE BUCI NIGHT

The clothes float slowly down, separating as they fall. RIMBAUD *watches calmly. Below, astonished, the crowd gapes up at the extraordinary vision.*

INT. MATHILDE'S BEDROOM NIGHT

MATHILDE *is in bed as* VERLAINE, *his mind still elsewhere, lets himself into the room.*

MATHILDE

Did you find him?

VERLAINE

I did.

MATHILDE

And did he give you back Daddy's crucifix?

VERLAINE *looks up at her sharply, his expression hardening.*

VERLAINE

If your father's capable of throwing that boy out without a penny, he's got no right to have Christ hanging all over his walls. You people don't understand what poverty is. Do you realise that in Charleville, if Rimbaud wanted a book, he had to go and steal it?

MATHILDE

That proves what kind of a person he is.

VERLAINE *bounds across the room, grabs her by the hair and drags her off the high bed. She hits the floor with a sickening crash. He stands over her as she struggles to her feet, then punches her in the face. She goes down again, knocking over the bedside table as she falls. She stays on the ground, moaning softly.* VERLAINE *starts forward and lifts her off the floor.*

VERLAINE

I'm sorry . . . I'm sorry, love . . . sorry. You shouldn't have said that.

He helps her over to the bed, at which point the door opens to reveal the
MAUTÉ DE FLEURVILLES, *both in their nightclothes, he in a nightcap and clutching a candle.*

MAUTÉ

What's going on? Mm?

MATHILDE

Nothing.

MAUTÉ

What was all that noise?

MATHILDE

I . . . knocked the table over.

MME MAUTÉ *hurries over and takes* MATHILDE *in her arms.*

MME MAUTÉ

Are you all right, dear?

MATHILDE *nods, very pale.* MAUTÉ *continues to glare at* VERLAINE.

MATHILDE

Yes. Yes, I'm all right.

INT. RIMBAUD'S ROOM IN THE RUE DE BUCI DAY

RIMBAUD *paces up and down, still naked, but wrapped in the coverlet from his mattress.* VERLAINE *sits in the single chair, watching him.*

RIMBAUD

So do you love her?

VERLAINE

Of course. She's ideal. Eighteen. Beautiful. Plenty of money.
All the wifely virtues. And she's about to give me a baby.

RIMBAUD

Do you have anything in common?

VERLAINE

No.

23

RIMBAUD

Is she intelligent?

VERLAINE

No.

RIMBAUD

Does she understand you?

VERLAINE

No.

RIMBAUD

So the only thing she can give you is sex?

Silence. They look at each other. Finally VERLAINE *rises to his feet.*

VERLAINE

Let me see if I can find you some clothes.

EXT. RUE NICOLET NIGHT

RIMBAUD *waits by the gate of the Mauté house. Presently, the door opens
and* VERLAINE *catapults out of the house.* RIMBAUD *opens the gate for
him.*

RIMBAUD

All right?

VERLAINE

For God's sake, let's have another drink.

EXT. BANKS OF THE SEINE DAY

VERLAINE *and* RIMBAUD *move along the Quai, deep in conversation.*

VERLAINE

We should do something about getting some of your work
published.

RIMBAUD

Why?

Why? Because that's what writers do.

Not me. I couldn't care less about being published. The only thing that matters is the writing itself. Everything else is literature.

He manages to imbue the last word with a memorable amount of contempt. VERLAINE, *perplexed, is searching for an answer to this when* RIMBAUD *goes on the attack.*

Your last book.

Yes?

It wasn't good enough.

You don't think so?

Premarital junk.

No, love poems. A lot of people found them very beautiful.

But they're lies.

They're not lies. I love her.

Love?

Yes.

No such thing.

What do you mean?

RIMBAUD

Whatever it is binds families and married couples together: that's not love. It's stupidity or selfishness or fear. Love doesn't exist.

VERLAINE

You're wrong.

RIMBAUD

Self-interest exists. Attachment based on personal gain exists. Complacency exists. But not love.

He stops for a moment, staring out across the brown water.

Love has to be reinvented.

INT. ANDRÉ'S NIGHT

The water trickles down once again over the sugar-lump into the absinthe. VERLAINE *finishes pouring and raises the glass to his lips.* RIMBAUD, *facing him, also raises his glass.*

RIMBAUD

Here's to your son.

INT. MATHILDE'S BEDROOM NIGHT

MATHILDE *wakes with a start as the door bursts open.* VERLAINE *stands in the doorway for a moment, swaying slightly, candle in hand. Then he advances unsteadily into the room.*

MATHILDE

Don't wake the baby.

VERLAINE

Never mind the baby.

He puts the candlestick down and pitches himself full-length onto the bed beside MATHILDE. *He kisses her and she submits to this, but a moment later, when he begins wrenching at her nightdress, she pulls herself away from him.*

26

MATHILDE

No.

VERLAINE

Why not? It's nearly a week since the baby was born.

He returns to the charge, but eventually MATHILDE *puts both hands on his chest and pushes him away as firmly as she can manage.*

MATHILDE

No!

VERLAINE *lets go of her abruptly, his eyes cold. Without a word, he picks up the pillow next to her and moves it to the bottom of the bed. Then he puts his head down on it, just as he is, hat, overcoat, muddy boots.*

The baby starts to cry. MATHILDE *stares miserably at the boots, a few inches away from her face.*

Fade.

EXT. VILLAGE IN THE ARDENNES DAY

LONG SHOT *of the village: a house is on fire, and a number of Prussian soldiers, in their striking uniforms, are rounding up the remaining villagers, mostly old people and children, and corralling them in a corner of the dusty square. The* SOUNDS *of guttural German commands in the distance.*

Over this, a caption:

II   FAUSSE CONVERSION

RIMBAUD (V.O.)

It was last summer, during the war.

Now we can see that this scene is from the P.O.V. *of* RIMBAUD, *who is lurking in the shadows on a hill which slopes down into the village. He watches for a moment, then turns to cut across a field in the direction of a wooded area.*

EXT. WOODS DAY

The CAMERA TRACKS *through woodland, pushing leaves aside as it goes.*

27

RIMBAUD (V.O.)
One of my times I ran away from home.

RIMBAUD *moves through the trees towards a blaze of distant light.*

EXT. CLEARING BY THE RIVER DAY

RIMBAUD *emerges into the brightly lit clearing, stops on the edge of the treeline, looking around. Mountains behind him in the distance.*

RIMBAUD (V.O.)
I came down to the river to fill my water bottle.

RIMBAUD *reacts suddenly, retreats back into the trees.*

HIS P.O.V.: *a* SOLDIER *is lying on the riverbank, dark blue and red uniform, apparently asleep.*

RIMBAUD (V.O.)
There was a Prussian soldier, not much older than me, asleep in a clearing.

INT. RIMBAUD'S ROOM IN THE RUE DE BUCI DAY

In the few weeks since RIMBAUD*'s arrival in Paris,* VERLAINE*'s appearance has changed drastically. He looks as if he's been wearing the same shabby clothes for several days.* RIMBAUD*'s hair has grown into a mane which cascades over his shoulders.*

RIMBAUD
I watched him for a long time before I realised: he wasn't asleep, he was dead. And somehow it clarified things for me.

EXT. CLEARING BY THE RIVER DAY

The dead SOLDIER *is smiling. He looks perfectly at ease except for a small pool of black blood issued from a neat wound just above his waist. Silence, except for the hum of insects. The surface of the river is fiercely bright.* RIMBAUD *sits beside the corpse, holding its hand.*

RIMBAUD (V.O.)

I understood that what I needed to become the first poet of
this century was to experience everything in my body. It was
no longer enough for me to be one person. I decided to be
everyone.

INT. RIMBAUD'S ROOM DAY

RIMBAUD *is staring piercingly at* VERLAINE.

RIMBAUD

I decided to be a genius. I decided to originate the future.

VERLAINE'*s face, as he considers this proposition.*

INT. CAFÉ DU THÉÂTRE DU BOBINO NIGHT

*A dinner of the Vilains Bonshommes, a poetry society, is in progress.
Food is being cleared away and the next stage, the poetry reading, is
about to begin. The featured poet this evening is* JEAN AICARD, *a portly
and respectable figure, now somewhat nervously sorting through his
papers.* VERLAINE *and* RIMBAUD *are sitting at a corner of the table at the
far end, both evidently somewhat the worse for drink. For some reason,*
RIMBAUD *is wearing a battered top hat. Their immediate neighbours at
the table are* CHARLES CROS *and the photographer* ÉTIENNE CARJAT,
*forty-three, a dapper figure with a goatee. Much of the following
dialogue is overlapped, forming part of the general buzz of animated
chatter.*

CROS

The principle is very like photography. Only instead of pho-
tographing a man's face, you photograph his voice.

RIMBAUD

For Christ's sake, let's get the fuck out of here.

VERLAINE

We can't.

RIMBAUD

Why not?

VERLAINE

He's just about to start reading.

CROS

Then, twenty years later, just as you might open a photograph album, you simply put the relevant cylinder into the paleophone and listen to him reading his poem or singing his song.

CARJAT

And you think you could invent a machine like that which worked?

CROS

Perfectly possible.

RIMBAUD

Which one is it?

VERLAINE

Aicard.

He points up towards the other end of the table.

Over there.

RIMBAUD

Oh, I don't think I'm going to like his stuff much.

VERLAINE *smiles at the understatement.*

CARJAT

What about your idea for colour photographs?

CROS

There's no money in it.

CARJAT *shakes his head, turns to* RIMBAUD, *who's in the process of demanding more wine from a passing waiter.*

CARJAT

I read those poems you left for me.

RIMBAUD

Oh, yes?

CARJAT

Remarkable. Very promising. Only it seems to me all that inge-
nuity is rather marred by . . . well, not exactly a juvenile urge to
shock, but something of the sort.

RIMBAUD

And were you shocked?

CARJAT

No, *I* wasn't, of course not.

RIMBAUD

Then why should you suppose I intended you to be?

CARJAT

Well . . . that's not really the point.

VERLAINE

Seems fair enough to me.

CARJAT

I could object to your technical approach.

RIMBAUD

I could object to your tie.

VERLAINE

He doesn't like discussing his poetry.

CARJAT

I see.

A ripple of applause as AICARD, *at the far end, rises to his feet.*

AICARD

Thank you, gentlemen. My first poem is written expressly for
children.

As he continues to speak, RIMBAUD *produces a small phial from his
waistcoat pocket and empties the contents into* CARJAT*'s wine, which
immediately begins to bubble and fizz.*

I would ask you to bear this in mind: although, as with all
worthwhile work for children, it is hoped that what is said is
not entirely without relevance to adults.

31

CARJAT *reaches for his wine, lifts it almost to his lips, then does a horrified double-take and puts the glass down hurriedly.* VERLAINE *suppresses a laugh, and* RIMBAUD *leans towards him with a murmured explanation.*

> RIMBAUD

Sulphuric acid.

At the other end of the table, AICARD *is clearing his throat.*

> AICARD

The poem is called "Green Absinthe."

A burst of ironic applause from RIMBAUD.

"Green absinthe is the potion of the damned . . ."

RIMBAUD *groans.*

"A deadly poison silting up the veins
While wife and child sit weeping in their slum . . ."

> RIMBAUD

I don't believe it.

A certain sensation. AICARD *decides to soldier on.*

> AICARD

"The drunkard pours absinthe into his brains."

> RIMBAUD

Shit.

> AICARD

"Oh! Drunkard, most contemptible of men . . ."

> RIMBAUD

Shit.

> AICARD

"Degraded, fallen, sinful and obtuse . . ."

His voice is beginning to crack.

> RIMBAUD

It is! It is! Authentic shit!

"Degraded, fallen, sinful and obtuse . . ."

RIMBAUD

I like it.

AICARD

"You scruple not to beat your wife and child . . ."

RIMBAUD

For trying to deprive you of the juice.

Pandemonium. Protests, laughter, shouting. AICARD *subsides hopelessly.* CARJAT *springs to his feet and turns on* RIMBAUD.

CARJAT

Get out, you!

RIMBAUD

Me?

CARJAT

Yes, you, you offensive little bastard. Get out, or I'll throw you out.

RIMBAUD

I think I may, may I not, be permitted to raise some objection against the butchering of French poetry?

CARJAT

No, you may not. Now apologise and get out.

He moves towards RIMBAUD, *who rises to his feet and grabs hold of* VERLAINE'*s walking stick.*

VERLAINE

Careful.

RIMBAUD

Don't come any nearer.

CARJAT

If you think you can frighten me with that thing . . .

He grabs hold of the walking stick; now RIMBAUD *pulls on it to reveal it's a swordstick. The blade flashes as* CARJAT *falls silent. Deadlock. They circle each other venomously. Then* CARJAT *lunges and* RIMBAUD *slashes out at him.* CARJAT, *appalled, cries out and grasps his wrist. Blood flows. Chaos.*

VERLAINE
Careful, I said.

But RIMBAUD *turns, pointing his sword at* AICARD.

RIMBAUD
And now, you!

He bears down on AICARD *who, for a moment, is transfixed with horror, before breaking and running for his life.* RIMBAUD *pursues him, slashing wildly at him.*

Fucking inkpisser!

Eventually, RIMBAUD *is overcome and disarmed.* VERLAINE *takes back the swordstick and breaks the blade over his knee. The incident appears to be over. But all of a sudden,* RIMBAUD *breaks free and jumps on the table.*

In the days of François Premier, wise and benevolent giants roamed the countryside. And one of their natural functions was to rid the world of pedants, fools and writers of no talent . . .

By now, before anyone can stop him, he's reached the top of the table, where he succeeds in pissing on AICARD's *poems and, when* AICARD *moves forward to try to rescue them, on* AICARD *himself.*

. . . by pissing on them from a great height!

EXT. RUE DE BUCI NIGHT

VERLAINE *and* RIMBAUD *make their way back, arm-in-arm, moving through the deserted streets, helpless with laughter.*

VERLAINE
How to make your way in the literary world.

34

RIMBAUD

What's depressing about this city is that the artists are even
more bourgeois than the fucking bourgeoisie.

They turn in through the narrow doorway of RIMBAUD*'s building.*

INT. RIMBAUD'S ROOM NIGHT

RIMBAUD *picks up the freshly lighted candle and lights the hashish and
tobacco mixture in his pipe.* VERLAINE *is already slumped in the chair,
watching him.* RIMBAUD *inhales luxuriously and then passes the pipe to*
VERLAINE.

RIMBAUD

Colour is what this gives you, colour. Thick colours you can
smell and hear. I'd like to go somewhere I could get it without
this.

He takes the pipe back from VERLAINE *and flops down on the mattress,
inhales again.*

South. Away from the dusty mantelpiece of Europe.

Dissolve.

INT. RIMBAUD'S ROOM DAWN

*The candle has burnt to a stub and guttered. Both men are in the same
position.* RIMBAUD *looks at* VERLAINE, *his eyes piercing.*

RIMBAUD

I think we should make a bargain. You help me and I'll help
you. If we go away together, I'm sure you'll be able to start
doing good work again. And when we've taken as much as we
can from one another, we split up and move on.

VERLAINE

How would we live?

RIMBAUD

You have some money.

35

VERLAINE

Ah. I understand. I help you by supporting you and you help
me by renewing my rusty old inspiration, is that it?

RIMBAUD

Not altogether.

RIMBAUD *rises abruptly from the mattress and stretches out a hand to*
VERLAINE. VERLAINE *hesitates through a long silence; then he gets up
and* RIMBAUD *takes him in his arms. A long kiss. The* CAMERA *rises
slowly away from them and back through the window.*

EXT. RUE DE BUCI DAY 1892

The same SHOT CONTINUES, *descending slowly to street level until it
picks out the older* VERLAINE. *He moves along the street blindly, limping
noticeably, in the grip of a violent emotion. A passer-by cannons into
him and unleashes a volley of abuse but neither he nor we hear it. He
comes to a ragged halt and stands in the street, tears gathering at the
corners of his eyes, the crowds parting about him as he looks up at the
blind window at the top of the building on the other side of the street,
remembering twenty years back.*

INT. OFFICES AT VANIER'S DAY

VERLAINE *trudges up a narrow staircase, through a large ante-office in
which an old printing press is in operation, past a frail-looking* WOMAN
*dressed in black, who sits on a bench waiting, and into a largely glassed-
in inner office where a* SECRETARY, *a severe-looking middle-aged
woman, sits behind a desk. He deposits the single piece of paper, on
which he's made a fair copy of his new poem, on the desk. The* SECRE-
TARY *takes it without comment, opens the petty cash box and counts out
five francs, which she hands over to him and which he pockets.*

SECRETARY

There's someone waiting to see you.

VERLAINE *follows the direction her eyes are indicating and sees, through
the glass, the frail* WOMAN *in black. He frowns, not recognising her.*

She didn't give a name.

36

Without more ado, VERLAINE *leaves the inner office and approaches the* WOMAN, *who sees him coming and rises to her feet.*

> WOMAN

Monsieur Verlaine?

> VERLAINE

I have a couple of appointments, I'm afraid, but perhaps we can make an arrangement to meet later, say early evening . . . ?

All this comes out with practised charm, as he's shaking the WOMAN'*s hand.*

> WOMAN

You don't remember me, do you? Here's my card.

She hands him a card. He glances down at it and then goes deathly pale. He looks back at the WOMAN, *his mouth opening and closing, and then, once again, down at the card.*

INSET: *The name on the card is* ISABELLE RIMBAUD; *quite clearly visible, even though* VERLAINE'*s hand is shaking.*

VERLAINE *looks up:* ISABELLE'*s calm face, from* HIS P.O.V.

EXT. RIMBAUD FARM AT ROCHE DAY 1872

CLOSE ON *a window in the main farm building: a waiflike child, dressed entirely in black, behind the window, stares out. This is, recognisably,* ISABELLE *at eleven. Suddenly, she reacts excitedly and disappears from the window.*

The CAMERA PULLS BACK *slowly to reveal the sombre facade of the Rimbaud family farm at Roche.*

The ensemble of eighteenth-century buildings is pleasant enough, but it sits on flat and featureless terrain, broken only by a few imposing poplars, and has been partially destroyed during the war. Outbuildings are half-collapsed, the walls blackened with fire and shell damage. The courtyard is overgrown with weeds. It's a bleak day in early spring.

As the CAMERA MOVEMENT *is completed,* RIMBAUD *strides into the courtyard, moving fast. At the same time, the main door of the farm-*

house is thrown open and the child rushes out and buries herself in his arms.

> RIMBAUD

Isabelle!

> ISABELLE

I didn't know you were coming.

In spite of her obvious excitement, there's something grave and pinched about her, as well as a maturity beyond her years.

> RIMBAUD

Where's the mouth of darkness?

> ISABELLE

Mother? She's in the fields with Vitalie. Do you want to see her?

RIMBAUD *shakes his head, his expression uncharacteristically tender.*

INT. HAYLOFT DAY

RIMBAUD *has arranged a rough table and wooden chair in the hayloft of one of the barns, so that the light passing through the opened shutters of a high window falls across it. He writes in a child's exercise book, with a scratchy child's pen, dipping it from time to time into a lead inkwell. All of a sudden, a shadow falls across the desk and he looks up.*

Standing above him is his MOTHER, *now forty-seven, although she looks older, lines of hardship etched into her unsmiling features. She's also dressed entirely in black.*

> MME RIMBAUD

Are you back for good?

> RIMBAUD

For good? I don't know. For better or worse.

> MME RIMBAUD

Because there's work to be done in the fields.

> RIMBAUD

There's work to be done here.

38

Silence. MME RIMBAUD *considers this for a while.*

> MME RIMBAUD
> I thought you were getting on well in Paris.

> RIMBAUD
> So I was. But Verlaine's wife started to make trouble.

> MME RIMBAUD
> What kind of trouble?

> RIMBAUD
> Threatening divorce, you know . . . she thought we were
> spending too much time together.

MME RIMBAUD *frowns in indignation.*

> MME RIMBAUD
> Spoilt rich girl, I suppose.

> RIMBAUD
> That's right.

> MME RIMBAUD
> This work you're doing: is it the kind of thing that will lead to
> anything?

> RIMBAUD
> I don't know. All the same, it's the kind of work I do.

There's another silence. Then MME RIMBAUD *turns and moves away.*

INT. FARMHOUSE KITCHEN DAY

MME RIMBAUD *sits at the head of a plain wooden table. On her right are
her sons, the older of whom,* FRÉDÉRIC, *although only eighteen, already
has the red face and broken veins of a confirmed drinker; on her left are
her daughters,* ISABELLE *and* VITALIE, *thirteen, a touchingly frail and
undersized child, alarmingly pale against her black dress.*

*It's still light outside, but the day is almost over. The meal is some kind of
vegetable stew.* RIMBAUD *grapples with his unenthusiastically. Except for
the clatter of cutlery, a profound silence reigns. Eventually,* FRÉDÉRIC

turns to RIMBAUD *and speaks, his voice gleeful, with a barely suppressed note of hysteria.*

FRÉDÉRIC

I don't suppose Paris ever gets as exciting as this?

EXT. FARMHOUSE AT ROCHE DAY

Blustery spring weather. RIMBAUD *strides away from the farmhouse, walking fast, carrying no luggage.*

Fade.

INT. MATHILDE'S BEDROOM NIGHT

VERLAINE *stands in the doorway, swaying slightly, candlestick in hand.*

Over this, a caption:

III   VIERGE FOLLE

VERLAINE'S P.O.V.: MATHILDE *lies in bed with* GEORGES *in her arms, a tableau of innocence. She wakes as* VERLAINE *advances into the room.*

VERLAINE

You look like a fucking saint.

He slams the candlestick down on the bedside table.

Except you haven't got a halo.

He leans over and wrenches GEORGES *from her arms.*

Where's your halo?

He turns and throws GEORGES *across the room. He means to throw him into his cradle but he misses. There's the usual moment of shocked silence before the baby's lungs begin to function and he begins a terrified howl.* MATHILDE *tries to scramble out of bed to attend to him, but* VERLAINE *holds her down.*

Come here. I'm going to give you your halo.

40

He hangs on to her and reaches for the candlestick. Then he holds the lighted candle to her hair. She remains perfectly still, her eyes tightly shut. The baby screams. Her hair smoulders and singes, but doesn't actually catch fire. VERLAINE *suddenly releases her, puts the candle down and bursts into tears.* MATHILDE *opens her eyes, speaks quietly.*

MATHILDE

He's back, isn't he?

INT. CAFÉ DU RAT MORT EVENING

A spectacularly dingy bar, even by VERLAINE'*s standards.*

RIMBAUD *picks at the blackened table with a large ugly knife.* VERLAINE *sits opposite, two empty glasses between them.* VERLAINE *waves at the* PATRON *standing stolidly behind the* zinc. *Otherwise, the place is more or less deserted.*

VERLAINE

Two more.

RIMBAUD

It's time we left.

VERLAINE

I've just ordered another drink.

RIMBAUD

Paris, Paris.

VERLAINE

Oh, no, I can't leave Mathilde at the moment, she's not very well.

RIMBAUD

I'm not surprised, if you keep setting fire to her.

VERLAINE

I haven't set fire to her since Thursday.

They both laugh.

It's not very funny.

41

They both laugh some more.

RIMBAUD

No, it's pathetic. Your acts of violence are always curiously disgusting.

VERLAINE

What do you mean?

RIMBAUD

They're not clean. You're always in some sort of drunken stupor. Then you start apologising and grovelling.

VERLAINE

I don't like hurting people.

RIMBAUD

Then don't. Or if you do, do it coolly and don't insult your victim by feeling sorry afterwards.

The PATRON arrives with the drinks. VERLAINE adds water to his, brooding silently for a while.

VERLAINE

I love her, you see.

RIMBAUD

You can't possibly.

VERLAINE

I love her body.

RIMBAUD

There are other bodies.

VERLAINE

No. I love Mathilde's body.

RIMBAUD

But not her soul?

VERLAINE

I think it's less important to love the soul than to love the body. After all, the soul may be immortal, we have plenty of time for the soul: but flesh rots.

42

RIMBAUD *snorts derisively.*

It's my love of flesh which keeps me faithful.

RIMBAUD

Faithful? What do you mean?

VERLAINE

I'm faithful to all my lovers, because once I love them, I will always love them. And when I'm alone in the evening or the early morning, I close my eyes and I celebrate them all.

RIMBAUD

That's not faithfulness, it's nostalgia. If you don't want to leave Mathilde, it's not because you are faithful, it's because you're weak.

VERLAINE

If strength involves brutality, I prefer to be weak.

RIMBAUD

With you, weakness involves brutality as well.

He looks angrily across at VERLAINE.

Don't expect me to be faithful to you.

VERLAINE

Why are you so harsh with me?

RIMBAUD

Because you need it.

VERLAINE

Isn't it enough for you to know that I love you more than I've ever loved anyone and that I'll always love you?

RIMBAUD

Shut up, you snivelling drunk.

VERLAINE

Tell me if you love me.

RIMBAUD

Oh, for God's sake . . .

Please.

RIMBAUD *looks away in disgust.* VERLAINE *reaches across the table and puts a hand on his arm.*

Please. It's important to me.

RIMBAUD *looks back at him, rage in his eyes.*

Please. Just say it.

RIMBAUD *lowers his eyes. He whittles away at the table.*

RIMBAUD
You know I'm very fond of you . . . we've been very happy sometimes. I . . .

He breaks off. Long silence. Eventually, he looks up at VERLAINE *and speaks, almost inaudibly.*

Do you love me?

VERLAINE
What?

RIMBAUD
Do you love me?

VERLAINE
Yes.

RIMBAUD
Then put your hands on the table.

VERLAINE
What?

RIMBAUD
Put your hands on the table.

VERLAINE *does so.*

Palm upwards.

VERLAINE *turns his hands palm upwards.* RIMBAUD *looks at them for a moment and then stabs at them both with short, brutal blows.* VERLAINE *sits looking at his hands in amazement as blood begins to drip down onto the floor. Finally,* RIMBAUD *speaks, with deadly quiet.*

The only unbearable thing is that nothing is unbearable.

INT. RIMBAUD'S ROOM IN THE RUE DE BUCI NIGHT

CLOSE *on* VERLAINE'S *hand, wrapped in a makeshift, bloodstained bandage, and his head, facedown on the bolster.*

RIMBAUD'S *face lunges* INTO FRAME, *and* VERLAINE *cries out as he's penetrated.*

Dissolve.

INT. RIMBAUD'S ROOM NIGHT

VERLAINE *and* RIMBAUD *stretched out on the mattress, seen in an* OVERHEAD SHOT, *in the bare, uncurtained moonlit room.* VERLAINE *comes up on one elbow, careful of his bandaged hands, and looks down at his sleeping friend.*

EXT. ABYSSINIAN PLATEAU DAY

A strange, jolting, TRACKING P.O.V. SHOT, *travelling across the cracked brown earth of some arid wilderness. A piece of white canvas flaps incongruously* IN *and* OUT OF SHOT.

INT. RIMBAUD'S ROOM NIGHT

VERLAINE *leans over towards* RIMBAUD. *Using the side of his bandaged hand, he brushes the hair out of* RIMBAUD'S *eyes with infinite care and tenderness.*

EXT. ABYSSINIAN PLATEAU DAY

Now the TRACKING SHOT *approaches a sheer drop, stops at the edge and settles. Below is a landscape of a scarcely imaginable austere ferocity: broken rock, fissured dark brown earth, no vegetation except for blackened thornbushes, dancing heat-haze, steep, jagged rock faces and bare*

plains featureless as a desert. Far below, shimmering at the edge of
FRAME, *the silver, dazzling stripe of some distant sea. There's no doubt
that this is Africa, if indeed it is anywhere on this planet.*

> RIMBAUD (V.O.)
> On. On.

INT. RIMBAUD'S ROOM NIGHT

RIMBAUD *moves restlessly in his sleep.*

> RIMBAUD
> On.

VERLAINE *watches, his eyes glittering in the moonlight.*

> VERLAINE (V.O.)
> How many hours have I watched beside his dear sleeping body,
> wondering why he wanted so much to escape from reality.
> There never was a man with such an aim. Did he perhaps
> know secrets *to change life?*

RIMBAUD*'s eyes open suddenly: pale and piercing.*

> RIMBAUD
> We have to leave.

> VERLAINE
> I don't know.

> RIMBAUD
> Yes, this is the time to leave, the summer. Happiest days of my
> life were last year when I ran away from home. No idea where I
> was, I just carried on. I've never known such long and coloured
> days. Only I never could get far enough. I've never seen the
> sea.

EXT. ABYSSINIAN PLATEAU DAWN

*The silver expanse of the sea, beyond which the sun's disc gradually
begins to appear. A slow* PANNING SHOT *begins to reveal the baked
brown of the arid edge of the plateau, as the sea's surface changes from
silver to gold.*

RIMBAUD (V.O.)

I wanted to walk to Africa and cross a desert. I wanted heat
and violence of landscape. I wanted the sun.

INT. RIMBAUD'S ROOM NIGHT

RIMBAUD *reaches up and takes* VERLAINE's *face between his hands.*

RIMBAUD

I want the sun. Do you understand?

VERLAINE

Yes.

*But like a dog, he can't sustain eye contact for long and looks away
shiftily.* RIMBAUD *releases him and slumps back on his pillow, sighing.*
VERLAINE *turns back to him, his expression tormented.*

EXT. RUE NICOLET DAY

Early morning on a blazing hot day. RIMBAUD *waits on a shady corner
of the street, watching the Mauté house.*

INT. MATHILDE'S BEDROOM DAY

VERLAINE, *formally dressed in frock-coat and wing-collar, bends over*
MATHILDE's *supine body, a hand on her brow, his expression concerned.
Not far off, the baby gurgles contentedly in his cradle.* MATHILDE *looks
flushed and feverish.*

VERLAINE

I'll go and fetch the doctor.

MATHILDE

No, you'll be late for work.

VERLAINE

Doesn't matter.

*He leans down to kiss her and moves off towards the door, glancing
back, his expression tender.*

I'll be right back.

47

EXT. RUE NICOLET DAY

RIMBAUD *watches* VERLAINE *emerging from the house, fetches a letter out of his pocket and sets off down the street, moving briskly, head down, so that* VERLAINE *has the impression he's seen him first.*

                    VERLAINE
Rimbe!

RIMBAUD *looks up, as if taken by surprise. Then he thrusts the letter at* VERLAINE.

                    RIMBAUD
Here.

                    VERLAINE
What's this?

                    RIMBAUD
I thought I'd say goodbye. I'm leaving Paris.

                    VERLAINE
When?

                    RIMBAUD
Now.

                    VERLAINE
Where are you going?

                    RIMBAUD
I don't know. Just away.

                    VERLAINE
I was just on my way to fetch a doctor. Mathilde's not well.

                    RIMBAUD
Why, what have you done to her?

                    VERLAINE
Nothing, it's a migraine.

                    RIMBAUD
Don't let me keep you.

But VERLAINE *doesn't move. He looks first one way, then the other, racked with indecision—*

Well, goodbye.

VERLAINE

Wait!

He closes his eyes, concentrating desperately: then opens them again.

I'm coming with you.

RIMBAUD

What about Mathilde?

VERLAINE *takes* RIMBAUD's *arm.*

VERLAINE

The hell with her, she'll survive.

They set off down the street, arm-in-arm.

EXT. BELGIAN COUNTRYSIDE DUSK

VERLAINE *and* RIMBAUD *jolt along in the back of an open cart. They're roaring with carefree laughter, passing a bottle of wine from hand to hand as the sun sets on an idyllic rural scene. The broad back of the* DRIVER *of the cart seems to provide them with complete privacy.*

RIMBAUD

You know, in Charleville I was a model pupil. All the prizes, top of the class. But I understood that wasn't enough, it was nothing. I wanted to disgust them as well as pleasing them. I knew how to take communion, now I wanted to take drugs. I decided on a long, systematic and conscientious course of debauchery. I needed to become someone else.

EXT. GARE DU MIDI, BRUSSELS NIGHT

VERLAINE *and* RIMBAUD *emerge from the station, a spring in their step.*

VERLAINE

This has always been my lucky town.

INT. ROOM IN THE HÔTEL DE COURTRAI, BRUSSELS DAWN

VERLAINE *and* RIMBAUD *lie entwined in the half-light in a large double
bed in a cheap hotel.* VERLAINE *extricates himself carefully and starts to
pull on his clothes.* RIMBAUD'*s eyes open, he's aware what's going on: but
when* VERLAINE *glances over in his direction, he closes his eyes again and
pretends to be asleep.*

EXT. HÔTEL LIÈGEOIS DAY

VERLAINE *stands, hesitating for a moment, outside what looks like a
much classier hotel than the one he's just left.*

INT. LOBBY OF THE HÔTEL LIÈGEOIS DAY

VERLAINE *moves authoritatively across the lobby and starts up the stairs
before the* CLERK *has time to register that his respectable clothes are
scuffed, crumpled and muddy.*

INT. CORRIDOR OF THE HÔTEL LIÈGEOIS DAY

VERLAINE *finds the door he's looking for, taps on it, gets no response, tries
the door and discovers it's open.*

INT. MATHILDE'S HOTEL ROOM DAY

VERLAINE *lets himself quietly into the room.* MATHILDE *is lying facedown
on the bed, naked, fast asleep.* VERLAINE *moves halfway across the room,
then stops to contemplate her, his mouth slightly open. A moment later,*
MATHILDE *wakes, senses his presence, jumps up, runs to him and buries
herself in his arms.*

MATHILDE

Paul!

They stand for a moment, locked in a passionate embrace. Then
VERLAINE *picks her up, carries her back to the bed, kicks off his shoes*

and lies down beside her, tearing off his clothes as fast as he can, with her enthusiastic assistance.

Dissolve.

Later; the two of them lie in each other's arms. He strokes her hair and kisses her.

VERLAINE

Do you remember happier times?

MATHILDE

Why did you leave us?

VERLAINE

I told you in my letter, I had a tip-off that I was going to be arrested for my work in the propaganda press, during the Commune.

MATHILDE

But that was over a year ago.

VERLAINE

The police may be slow, but they're methodical. I couldn't bear to go to jail. So I think it's best if I stay out of the country for a few months.

MATHILDE

With Rimbaud.

VERLAINE

Well . . .

MATHILDE

I suppose he's wanted by the police as well.

VERLAINE

No . . .

MATHILDE

Why do you prefer him to me?

VERLAINE

I don't, my love, I don't.

Silence. MATHILDE *moves away from him and leaves the bed. She moves across to where her clothes are neatly laid out, pours some water into the nearby basin, washes herself and begins to get dressed.*

You don't have to get dressed right away, do you?

MATHILDE

I told Mummy I'd meet her for breakfast.

VERLAINE

What's she doing here?

MATHILDE

She came with me.

VERLAINE

Well, that's another thing: I certainly can't stand living with your parents anymore.

MATHILDE

It's not safe anywhere else.

VERLAINE

What do you mean?

MATHILDE

You know what I mean.

Silence. VERLAINE *avoids her eye. She comes over and sits on the bed. He reaches up to stroke her shoulders and neck.*

Listen, I had this idea, I thought of this idea. I thought we might emigrate.

VERLAINE

Emigrate? Where to?

MATHILDE

New Caledonia. A lot of your friends from the Commune are out there. You'd be able to write. It'd be like it was when we were first married and . . .

VERLAINE

What?

52

MATHILDE

Nothing.

VERLAINE

No; go on.

MATHILDE

I was only going to say: you could stop . . . it would be easier
for you . . . if you wanted . . . to stop drinking.

VERLAINE

You're frightened of me, aren't you?

She doesn't answer; he takes her in his arms.

Don't think I like getting drunk. I mean, I do like getting
drunk, but I don't like being drunk. Or anyway, when I hit
your or . . . I feel so terrible about it, the only thing I can think
of is to get drunk again and forget about it. Most of the time I
want to give it up as much as you want me to. But it's as diffi-
cult as deciding to wake up when you're asleep. Perhaps I
could wake up out there. Can you see us living in a grass hut or
whatever they have?

MATHILDE

Why not?

VERLAINE

Then let's go, for Christ's sake, let's go. Before it's too late.

MATHILDE

We can go whenever you like.

VERLAINE

God, I love you.

He kisses her, a long, clinging kiss, after which he begins to undress her. But she pulls away from him.

MATHILDE

Not now.

VERLAINE

Why not?

She doesn't answer; instead she steps into her stern, billowing dress.

MATHILDE

Help me with this.

VERLAINE *grudgingly concedes and helps her. He takes her in his arms; and now, with him naked and her dressed, they form a reverse image to the opening of the scene.*

INT. CORRIDOR IN THE HÔTEL LIÈGEOIS DAY

MATHILDE *leaves the room and sets off down the corridor: only to come to a halt with a sudden gasp.* ANOTHER ANGLE *reveals, leaning against the wall, blocking her way, his expression sardonic:* RIMBAUD.

MATHILDE

Why are you doing this to us?

RIMBAUD

Don't worry, you can have him back quite soon: and only slightly damaged.

MATHILDE

He's coming back now.

She stands her ground, facing him down defiantly. They look at each other for a moment and then MATHILDE *pushes past* RIMBAUD, *leaving him not quite as confident as she found him.*

INT. MATHILDE'S HOTEL ROOM DAY

VERLAINE *starts up in bed as* RIMBAUD *barges into the room.*

> RIMBAUD

I see.

> VERLAINE

What are you doing here?

> RIMBAUD

Nice, was it? A scene of conjugal bliss?

> VERLAINE

I'm going back to Paris with her.

> RIMBAUD

Right.

55

He turns on his heel and heads for the door so abruptly that VERLAINE *has to speak fast to interrupt him.*

VERLAINE
No, wait, wait, let me explain.

RIMBAUD
Why should I?

VERLAINE
It's not what you think. It's something else. She suggested that we emigrate.

RIMBAUD
Emigrate?

VERLAINE
Yes, to New Caledonia. It'd be a change for me, a quiet life, I could stop drinking, don't you think it's a good idea?

RIMBAUD
No.

VERLAINE
You don't care about my happiness, do you?

RIMBAUD
No, and neither should you.

Silence. VERLAINE *shakes his head in confusion.*

VERLAINE
You've never been able to understand how much I love her. I walked in this morning and she was lying there, naked, on the bed. She looked so beautiful, she looked so young and con-fused. . . .

He breaks off, aware that RIMBAUD *is laughing.*

What's so funny?

RIMBAUD
Was she really lying naked on the bed?

VERLAINE
Yes.

RIMBAUD

Well, my estimation for her goes up a long way.

VERLAINE

What do you mean? Why?

RIMBAUD

For realising what was required and providing it.

He shakes his head, suddenly impatient.

Oh, what's it matter? She's your wife, you love her, go back to her.

He strides out of the room

INT. CORRIDOR IN THE HÔTEL LIÈGEOIS DAY

As RIMBAUD *walks down the corridor, away from the* CAMERA, *he reaches up to where the wallpaper has begun to come away from the wall a little and without breaking stride he rips away the entire sheet of wallpaper.*

INT. TRAIN COMPARTMENT DAY

VERLAINE *sits opposite* MATHILDE *and* MME MAUTÉ, *his expression morose.*

MATHILDE

Daddy says he's more than willing to help with the fares to New Caledonia.

VERLAINE *looks up, sharply.*

VERLAINE

Oh, so this is all his idea, is it?

MME MAUTÉ

As a matter of fact, it was my idea. But if you prefer to stay in Paris, of course, no one would be happier than I.

VERLAINE *relaxes again. He turns and stares gloomily out of the window.*

57

EXT.   STATION AT QUIÉVRAIN   DAY

*At the Franco-Belgian border, everyone's papers have to be stamped.
The passengers who've undergone this process mill around, eventually
drifting back onto the train. Another train waits on the facing platform.*
GUARDS *shout inaudible announcements.* VERLAINE *is shepherding*
MATHILDE *and* MME MAUTÉ *back onto the train. As he waits for them
to climb aboard, he looks up and sees something.*

VERLAINE'S P.O.V.: *standing on the bridge between the platforms,
wreathed in smoke, is* RIMBAUD. *He's standing quite motionless, staring
down at* VERLAINE, *his expression grave.*

> VERLAINE
> I'm just going to find a newspaper.

> MME MAUTÉ
> Don't be long.

VERLAINE *grunts an acknowledgement and moves off down the platform. After a few paces he stops, looking up again at the bridge between
the platforms, agonised. There's no sign of* RIMBAUD. *The engine on the
facing platform gives a couple of premonitory blasts of steam, and*
VERLAINE, *as if suddenly galvanised, makes a dash for the bridge and
races across to the other side, holding on to his hat as he runs.*

INT.   TRAIN COMPARTMENT   DAY

MATHILDE *and* MME MAUTÉ *are settled in their compartment, when the
train facing them begins to move. They pay very little attention to this,
until suddenly something catches their eye and they both react, appalled.*

Their P.O.V.: *in the other train, moving away from them now, is*
VERLAINE, *his tongue sticking out and his thumbs in his ears, making
an obscenely insolent face at them. Again, no sign of* RIMBAUD.

MATHILDE *and* MME MAUTÉ *look at each other, scarcely able to believe
what they've just seen.*

When they look back, it's in time to catch a glimpse of RIMBAUD, *who is
now standing next to* VERLAINE, *also wildly grimacing.*

As her train starts and begins to jolt out of the station, MATHILDE, in a
sudden access of rage, grabs VERLAINE's carpetbag and hurls it out of the
window.

INT. TRAIN COMPARTMENT (SECOND TRAIN) DAY

VERLAINE and RIMBAUD collapse onto the seats opposite one another,
shaking with helpless laughter.

INT. BELGIAN COUNTRYSIDE DAY

The train pulls away, out into the open countryside.

Fade.

EXT. BELGIAN COAST DAY

Summer's day. VERLAINE leads RIMBAUD up a narrow path rising
through grassland. At the last minute, impatient, RIMBAUD overtakes
him, arriving first at the crest of the headland and stopping dead.

REVERSE SHOT: RIMBAUD stands, his eyes sparkling, an expression of
wonder. VERLAINE comes up alongside him, says something and makes a
proprietorial gesture as if he's personally responsible for the view.

It's by no means a spectacular view, the greyish expanse of the English
Channel, the waves lapping timidly onto a pebble beach. But it's obvi-
ously RIMBAUD's first view of the sea and his excitement is palpable.

Over this, a caption:

IV   ALCHIMIE DU VERBE

EXT. PLOUGHED FIELDS DAY

The sun blazes down: this time it's VERLAINE who follows RIMBAUD
as he marches across the fields in the middle of a vast tract of open
countryside.

RIMBAUD (V.O.)
The first thing he did, it seems, when he was given the ring—a
magic ring, you understand—was to summon up a beautiful

59

woman, the most beautiful he could imagine. And they were
wonderfully happy and lived alone on a light blue southern
island.

EXT. RIVERBANK DUSK

VERLAINE *and* RIMBAUD *sit, passing a bottle of wine from hand to hand,
leaning against the broad trunk of an elm, as the sun starts to go down
behind a distant church spire. Somewhere, a bell tolls the angelus.*

> RIMBAUD (V.O.)
> One day he explained to her that with the ring he could grant
> her anything she wanted; and she asked him to build her a city.
> So he caused a city to grow up out of the sea, full of churches
> and echoing courtyards.

EXT. COUNTRY ROAD NIGHT

VERLAINE *and* RIMBAUD *lie huddled in a dry ditch beside a deserted
road, in each other's arms.*

61

RIMBAUD (V.O.)
She was so delighted with it that he granted her another wish,
and she asked for a ship. So he gave her a magnificent galleon
which needed no crew to look after the silk hangings and
golden figurehead.

EXT. FARMLAND DAY

*As the mist clears from the fields, RIMBAUD uproots a couple of turnips,
shakes the earth off, hands one to VERLAINE and bites into the other.*

RIMBAUD (V.O.)
It seemed to give her such happiness that he decided to grant
her one more wish. "One more wish," he said, "I will grant you
one more wish." "Give me the ring," she said.

EXT. BEACH DAY

*RIMBAUD sits at the end of a deserted jetty. Beside him is a small heap of
pebbles, which, one by one, he's throwing out to sea. VERLAINE stands
nearby, watching him.*

RIMBAUD (V.O.)

He gave it to her. She smiled serenely at him and threw it into
the sea. At once, she disappeared, the ship disappeared and the
city slowly sank back under the water.

EXT. DECK OF A FERRY BOAT NIGHT

VERLAINE *and* RIMBAUD *sit huddled on the upper deck of the Ostend-
Dover ferry. The ship is pitching in a swell, the wind is gusty and the
deck is otherwise deserted, as* RIMBAUD *finishes his story.*

RIMBAUD

For a long time after that the man sat looking out to sea without moving. Finally, he began to weep, because he understood
what he had done and that he would be alone forever. That was
it. Something like that.

EXT. ENGLISH CHANNEL DAWN

VERLAINE *and* RIMBAUD *lean over the deck-rail, as seagulls dip and call
harshly and a grey dawn breaks.*

THEIR P.O.V.: *rising theatrically sheer, the white cliffs of Dover.*

INT. ANDRÉ'S EVENING 1892

ISABELLE RIMBAUD *looks up from some papers she has spread out on one
of the bar's better-lit shabby tables and sees* VERLAINE *limping towards
her. She rises to her feet, her expression guarded, though not unfriendly.
They shake hands.*

VERLAINE

Please sit down, please. Has André been looking after you?
Can I get you something to drink?

ISABELLE

No, thank you.

VERLAINE

I think I might, just to celebrate this remarkable encounter. Do
you mind?

ISABELLE

Not at all.

VERLAINE *waves a hand and* ANDRÉ, *the mountainous patron, brings the already prepared absinthe to him at once.* VERLAINE *pours the water over the sugar-lump with barely concealed impatience.*

VERLAINE

You look a bit like him, you know. Your eyes are not unlike his.

ISABELLE

So I've been told.

VERLAINE *takes a long draught of absinthe;* ISABELLE *straightens the papers in front of her and draws from among them a book.*

It's really a business matter I want to discuss with you, Monsieur Verlaine.

VERLAINE

I'm at your service, Mademoiselle.

She indicates the book in her hand. It's called Le Réliquaire.

ISABELLE

This was published a few months ago; a completely unauthorised selection of my brother's poems. My mother and I were extremely upset.

VERLAINE *is very uncomfortable; it's quite clear he knows more about this than* ISABELLE *suspects.*

VERLAINE

I've seen it, yes.

ISABELLE

My mother and I are anxious to prevent anything like this from happening again. We thought you might be able to help us.

VERLAINE

I? How?

ISABELLE

I understand you have a large number of my brother's manuscripts.

66

VERLAINE

I have . . . some, yes.

ISABELLE

Well, my mother and I would be very grateful if you would
return them.

VERLAINE *looks away, avoiding* ISABELLE*'s eye.*

VERLAINE

I've always tried to use . . . the utmost discretion in everything
concerning your brother. I think I can say I've always defended
his interests. Sometimes I wonder why, since in many ways
they're diametrically opposed to my own.

ISABELLE

I don't see how. In what way?

VERLAINE

It took many years for your brother's work to be understood:
but once his name began to be well known, it soon became
clear *our* days were numbered. The music of old-fashioned
verse was no longer enough. He swept us away. Not that I
mind, you understand. I know I was once a good writer.

ISABELLE

I didn't know his name was so well known.

VERLAINE

Yes.

ISABELLE *frowns, grappling with the implications of this new informa-
tion.*

INT. BED-SITTING ROOM AT 34 HOWLAND ST.,
LONDON DAY 1872

RIMBAUD *and* VERLAINE*'s London lodgings are formed from the
drawing-room of a once elegant Georgian house on the fringes of Soho.
There's a desk in the window at which* RIMBAUD *is sitting, thinking,
occasionally scribbling a few words in the notebook in front of him.
Tranquil domestic atmosphere.*

VERLAINE (V.O.)

And what matters to me is that we did our best work together, both of us.

During this, VERLAINE *has wandered over to* RIMBAUD*'s desk and picked up his notebook. He reads silently for a moment, then decides to read aloud.*

VERLAINE

"I became a fabulous opera: I saw that all creatures are condemned to happiness: action is not life, but a means of squandering strength, a wearing down. Morality is intellectual weakness."

RIMBAUD

Well, it is, isn't it?

VERLAINE *turns the page and reacts with surprise.*

VERLAINE

What's this? Are you going back to rhymes?

He reads out again.

"I have researched the magic shapes
Of the happiness no one escapes."

He looks up.

That's wonderful. What does it mean?

RIMBAUD *doesn't answer; instead he reaches out and gently reclaims his
notebook.* VERLAINE *shakes his head admiringly.*

Why did you choose me to write to? I've often wondered.
You're so far up ahead, I can't even understand the signs
you're making. You make me feel I'm from another century. "I
have researched the magic shapes of the happiness no one
escapes."

RIMBAUD

I chose you for a very good reason. I've always known what to
say; but you, you know how to say. I thought I could learn from
you: and I have.

VERLAINE *is very pleased: he puts his arm round* RIMBAUD *and kisses
him on the cheek.*

EXT. HYDE PARK DUSK

It's foggy and the bare trees indicate that winter is now well advanced.
RIMBAUD *and* VERLAINE *stroll together, the latter exaggeratedly wrapped
up against the cold with overcoat, red scarf wrapped around his nose
and cotton wool in his ears. Around them, the lovers, the nannies with
their perambulators, the smartly dressed riders on their handsome horses.
The sun is a red ball seen through a lattice of bare branches.*

RIMBAUD

What's your greatest fear?

VERLAINE

I don't know, I wouldn't like to mislay my balls. Why, what's
your greatest fear?

RIMBAUD

That other people will see me as I see them.

69

They pass through the gates, moving towards the group of orators on their soap-boxes, surrounded by drifting audiences.

VERLAINE

One evening, did I ever tell you, I set out to assassinate Napoleon III. I was rather drunk and I decided things had gone far enough. Unfortunately, I never managed it.

RIMBAUD *smiles at him with some tenderness, takes his arm.*

Of course, here they have the famous democracy.

They drift on, arm-in-arm.

INT. PUB IN SOHO DAY

A smoke-filled, cavernous pub, sawdust on the floor, crowded with a cos-mopolitan clientèle, many of them refugees from one European country or another, most of them on the edge of poverty. VERLAINE *brings* RIMBAUD *a pint of beer, which* RIMBAUD *samples, grimacing as he does so.*

VERLAINE

No absinthe. Just this warm piss.

RIMBAUD

I like it.

VERLAINE

We're getting quite short of money, you know.

RIMBAUD

So you keep saying.

VERLAINE

Perhaps it's time we took a job.

RIMBAUD

I've told you before, I've no intention of taking a job. My work's going too well, I can't afford to waste time earning money.

He's said this quite simply and VERLAINE *laughs at the outrageousness of it.*

INT. BRITISH MUSEUM READING ROOM DAY

RIMBAUD *is escorted to his desk by a frock-coated* LIBRARIAN. *He nods in acknowledgement and sits. For a moment, he looks around, up at the great dome which gives the room its cathedral-like immensity and at the* READERS, *disposed each at his or her individual space or roaming the walkways above in search of reference works.*

RIMBAUD *reaches for his notebook, opens it, takes up his pen.*

EXT. DOCKS DAY

RIMBAUD *and* VERLAINE *move along the quaysides, teeming with sailors of all nationalities. Piles of crates block the way, where ships are loading and unloading and impromptu marketplaces are thronged with haggling Eastenders. The Thames is wide here and iron-grey.* RIMBAUD *seems intensely fascinated with the life around him.* VERLAINE, *preoccupied, breaks into his reverie.*

> VERLAINE
> I had a letter this morning. From Mathilde's lawyer.

> RIMBAUD
> And?

> VERLAINE
> She's applied for a legal separation on the grounds that you
> and I are "indulging in immoral relations."

> RIMBAUD
> Is that so?

> VERLAINE
> And he wants to know if we're prepared to submit to a medical
> examination.

> RIMBAUD
> What?

> VERLAINE
> I don't know what makes them think they can make that kind
> of outrageous accusation.

71

RIMBAUD

Wait a minute . . .

VERLAINE

I'm going to write straight back, I'm going to say as far as we're concerned, the whole gang of them can look up our asses.

RIMBAUD *looks at him for a moment, incredulous.*

RIMBAUD

What are you, insane?

He's spoken with some vehemence, but he can't take this very seriously and now he stops walking, his eye distracted by a ship which is preparing to cast off, its decks crowded with lascars. On the stern, beneath the ship's name, is printed its port of origin: BATAVIA.

Batavia. You can hear the wind rustling in the palm trees.

EXT. ABYSSINIAN PLATEAU DAY

Another strange, jerky TRACKING SHOT. *The piece of canvas flaps* IN *and* OUT OF SHOT.

INT. BED-SITTING ROOM IN HOWLAND ST. NIGHT

VERLAINE *wakes and looks down, concerned, at* RIMBAUD *as he thrashes about in the big wooden-framed bed.*

RIMBAUD

On. On.

EXT. ABYSSINIAN PLATEAU DAY

Once again, the dizzying panorama of the Abyssinian coastal plain. As the SHOT SETTLES, *the* SOUNDS *of the tropics begin to establish themselves.*

RIMBAUD (V.O.)

On!

72

INT. BED-SITTING ROOM NIGHT

RIMBAUD *wakes with a start, to find* VERLAINE *looking down at him.*

VERLAINE
Are you all right?

RIMBAUD
Just a dream.

VERLAINE
Shall I make some tea?

RIMBAUD *shakes his head: there's a strange, remote expression in his eyes.*

RIMBAUD
Do you think we should move on?

VERLAINE
You mean . . . ?

RIMBAUD
I mean, what about Mathilde's lawyer? Shouldn't we escape?

VERLAINE
Oh no, don't worry about that. But we will have to move from here. I can't afford it anymore; so yesterday, while you were at the museum, I found us another place.

INT. BED-SITTING ROOM AT 8 GREAT COLLEGE ST., LONDON DAY

A far drabber and more cramped room, this time in Camden Town. The window, on the first floor, looks down on a dispiriting street of terraced houses. RIMBAUD *is standing at the window, staring out at the grey skies, the drizzle and the shiny wet street.* VERLAINE *is finishing unpacking; more or less distracted by this, he's not paying a great deal of attention to* RIMBAUD.

RIMBAUD
You don't seem at all worried about this divorce.

VERLAINE
They're not going to give her a divorce. It's just sabre-rattling.

73

RIMBAUD

They can give it to her on desertion, you know. And if it's
desertion and sodomy, they can throw us both in jail as well.

He looks back into the room.

I'm not going to jail.

VERLAINE

I don't know: would it be so bad?

He's not taking the conversation at all seriously. RIMBAUD*'s expression,
on the other hand, is sombre.*

INT. BRITISH MUSEUM READING ROOM DAY

RIMBAUD *sits at his desk, dwarfed by the vast proportions of the room. He
crouches over a blank sheet of paper, frowning ferociously, his fist clenched.*

EXT. GREAT COLLEGE ST. DAY

It's raining again. VERLAINE, *carrying a bag of groceries, lets himself
into the house.*

INT. BED-SITTING ROOM DAY

RIMBAUD *is sitting at the table, his face buried in his arms. He doesn't stir
as* VERLAINE *comes in to the room and puts down his bag of groceries.*

VERLAINE

What's the matter?

RIMBAUD *raises his head and turns to look at him.*

RIMBAUD

It's so hard. Who would have imagined it would be so hard?

INT. PUB IN SOHO EVENING

VERLAINE *and* RIMBAUD *sit at a corner table, pints of "ordinary" in
front of them.*

VERLAINE

I wrote to the lawyer today: I explained to him, it's her father who's in the wrong. How many times have I asked for my things back from that house? And he takes no notice whatsoever.

RIMBAUD

You're in the wrong.

VERLAINE*'s jaw clenches in sudden cold anger.*

VERLAINE

All right, I'm in the wrong, if you say so, then that's established, isn't it?

RIMBAUD *doesn't answer. For a moment* VERLAINE *sulks, his mouth a thin line. Then he turns to* RIMBAUD.

I don't know, what is it? You seem different.

RIMBAUD

Yes. It's the writing. The writing has changed me.

And he does, indeed, look different. They sit on, in silence.

Fade.

INT. READING ROOM OF THE BRITISH MUSEUM DAY 1873

RIMBAUD *sits at his desk, as if in a trance, still in front of a blank piece of paper. Finally, he picks up his pen and writes something at the top of the page.*

INSERT: *What he writes, in capital letters, is:* L'IMPOSSIBLE.

Over this, a caption:

V L'IMPOSSIBLE

He puts down his pen and stares at the paper for some time.

OVERHEAD SHOT: RIMBAUD *at his desk.*

Suddenly, to the absolute horror of everyone else in the reading room, he throws back his head and utters a long-drawn-out, blood-curdling animal cry, somewhere between a howl and a groan.

After a moment of frozen shock, from different directions, various frock-coated museum OFFICIALS *begin to converge on his desk.*

INT. BED-SITTING ROOM IN GREAT COLLEGE ST. DAY

VERLAINE *stands at the window opening a bottle of wine, looking out on a sunless but oppressively warm grey day. He draws the cork and turns to look at* RIMBAUD, *who lies in bed between grubby sheets, completely immobile.*

VERLAINE
Any chance of you moving about at all today?

RIMBAUD
How long have we been in this shit-hole?

VERLAINE
Not more than five weeks.

RIMBAUD
God, life will never end.

VERLAINE *pours wine into two glasses, takes one over to* RIMBAUD.

VERLAINE
A lot can happen in five weeks.

RIMBAUD
A lot can happen in ten minutes. But it rarely does.

He gulps down the wine and holds out his glass.

More.

VERLAINE *fills his glass.*

VERLAINE
You have to shake yourself out of this depression, inertia, whatever it is. There's nothing preventing us from being happy
again.

RIMBAUD
I've told you before, I'm far too intelligent to be happy.

INT. PUB IN SOHO DAY

RIMBAUD, *clearly in a state of inner ferment, stares at his glass;*
VERLAINE *is drinking his beer. A thought strikes him and he speaks*
with a kind of forced cheerfulness.

> VERLAINE
>
> Do you realise I shall be thirty next birthday? What a horrible
> thought.

RIMBAUD *looks up, his gaze unseeing.*

> RIMBAUD
>
> I'm in despair.

VERLAINE *is surprised by this, but not as surprised as one might expect.*

> VERLAINE
>
> Why?

> RIMBAUD
>
> When I was young and golden and infallible, I saw the future
> with some clarity. I knew it would be difficult, but I thought
> that all I needed was experience and I could turn myself into
> the philosopher's stone and create new colours and new
> flowers, new languages and a new God and everything to gold.
> But now I find I've tormented myself and poked among my
> entrails to discover something that people do not believe or do
> not wish to believe or would be foolish to believe. There's no
> love in the world and no hope and I can do nothing about it.
> And I'm in hell.

Abruptly, he gets up and hurries out of the pub. VERLAINE *struggles to*
his feet and follows.

EXT. PUB DAY

VERLAINE *emerges from the pub, looking one way, then another.*

HIS P.O.V.: RIMBAUD *is running away, moving fast through the summer*
rain.

VERLAINE *sets off after him, but quite soon, as* RIMBAUD *vanishes around*
a corner, he gives up and comes to a halt, panting and dishevelled.

RIMBAUD *lies on the bed, fully clothed.* VERLAINE *is at the desk, trying to write.*

RIMBAUD

I suppose you think I've just been lying here all these weeks in a state of paralysed sloth.

VERLAINE

Well, not necessarily . . .

RIMBAUD

Well, I have. But bubbling beneath the surface and rising slowly through the layers of indifference has been a new system. Harden up. Reject romanticism. Abandon rhetoric. Get it right. And finally I've seen where my attempt to conquer the world has led me.

VERLAINE

And where has it led you?

RIMBAUD

Here. My search for universal experience has led me here. To lead an idle, pointless life of poverty, as the minion of a bald, ugly, ageing, drunken lyric poet, who clings onto me because his wife won't take him back.

Sickening silence. VERLAINE *gapes at* RIMBAUD, *for a moment too astonished to speak.*

VERLAINE

How can you bring yourself to say a thing like that?

RIMBAUD

It's easy. It's the truth. You're here, living like this, because you have to be. It's your life. Drink and sex and a kind of complacent melancholy and enough money to soak yourself oblivious every night. That's your limit. But I'm here because I choose to be.

VERLAINE

Oh, yes?

78

RIMBAUD

Yes.

VERLAINE

And why exactly? Why did you choose to come to London
with me? No doubt you regarded it as another stage in your
private odyssey. Only by plunging ever deeper, if I may mix
my myths, will you attain the right to graze on the upper
slopes of Parnassus.

Silence. RIMBAUD *seems to have decided to ignore* VERLAINE.

Of course, there are less subtle reasons for your putting up
with me.

RIMBAUD

Such as?

VERLAINE

Such as the fact that I support you.

RIMBAUD *raises his head to look at* VERLAINE *before speaking, icy and
venomous.*

RIMBAUD

Your mind is almost as ugly as your body.

They look at each other. VERLAINE *struggles with himself for a moment,
then his face suddenly goes blank. He rises to his feet and heads for the
door.*

Where are you going?

VERLAINE *ignores the question and leaves the room, slamming the door
behind him.* RIMBAUD*'s face is set in a mask of cold indifference.*

EXT. GREAT COLLEGE ST. DAY

VERLAINE *rounds the corner, his expression preoccupied. He's carrying a
herring in one hand and a bottle of oil in the other. He looks up as he
approaches the house to see* RIMBAUD *sitting in the open window of their
room. He's laughing.* VERLAINE *comes to a halt and looks up at him, his
face flushing.*

INT./EXT. BED-SITTING ROOM DAY

RIMBAUD *laughs, looking down at the absurd figure of* VERLAINE, *below in the street, with his herring and his bottle of oil.*

EXT. GREAT COLLEGE ST. DAY

VERLAINE *stands, looking up at* RIMBAUD, *who now leans out of the window to speak.*

                              RIMBAUD
    God, you look such a cunt.

INT./EXT. BED-SITTING ROOM DAY

RIMBAUD'S P.O.V.: VERLAINE *suddenly draws back his arm and hurls the bottle of oil at the window.*

RIMBAUD *flinches as the bottle smashes against the wall of the house.*

EXT. GREAT COLLEGE ST. DAY

VERLAINE *hurls the herring at the house as well. Then he turns and sets off back down the road.* RIMBAUD *leans out of the window again.*

                              RIMBAUD
    Where are you going?

INT./EXT. BED-SITTING ROOM DAY

RIMBAUD *watches the receding figure of* VERLAINE *for a moment. Then he calls out again, an edge of panic in his voice.*

                              RIMBAUD
    Where are you going?

VERLAINE *doesn't turn.* RIMBAUD, *who all of a sudden looks frightened and vulnerable, hurries out of the door.*

EXT. DOCKS DAY

RIMBAUD, *clearly in a panic, is running along the quay towards St. Katherine's Dock, streaming with sweat, cannoning into unwary passers-by, moving as fast as he can.*

An OVERHEAD SHOT *shows the gangways being drawn up on the Antwerp ferry as the engines begin to churn, while the small figure of* RIMBAUD, *hair billowing out behind him, races along the quayside towards the ship.*

As RIMBAUD *arrives alongside the ship, it's just beginning to pull away from the quay. He's hardly able to get his breath, but he can see* VERLAINE, *who is standing at the handrail looking down at him, his expression blank and sombre.*

> RIMBAUD
> Don't go! Come back! Don't leave me!

VERLAINE *puts his head to one side and makes no response.*

> I'm sorry.

Still not a flicker of acknowledgement from VERLAINE.

> How am I supposed to live?

At this VERLAINE *simply turns his back and moves off into the shadows of the deck until he disappears.* RIMBAUD, *his calm for once entirely shattered, buries his face in his hands and begins to sob.*

INT. BED-SITTING ROOM NIGHT

The room is lit only by the ghostly secondary light thrown by the gas-lamps out in the street. RIMBAUD *sits on the floor, leaning against the wall, one knee drawn up, his face a mask of despair.*

Over this, RIMBAUD'S *voice, full of frantic, childlike appeal.*

> RIMBAUD (V.O.)
> Come back, come back, you're my only friend. I promise I'll behave myself.

EXT. HÔTEL LIÈGEOIS

VERLAINE *stands outside the hotel, hesitating for a moment.*

> RIMBAUD (V.O.)
> It was only a stupid joke, I can't tell you how sorry I am.

INT. LOBBY OF THE HÔTEL LIÈGEOIS

VERLAINE *signs the register under the beady eye of the* CLERK, *who clearly doesn't approve much of clients without luggage.*

> RIMBAUD (V.O.)
> Come back and we'll forget all about it. It was only a joke.

INT. CORRIDOR IN THE HÔTEL LIÈGEOIS DAY

VERLAINE *hesitates in front of the door to the room he's been assigned: he recognises it as the room* MATHILDE *had the previous year.*

> RIMBAUD (V.O.)
> I haven't stopped crying for two days. When I called to you, why didn't you get off the boat?

INT. ROOM IN THE HÔTEL LIEGÈOIS DAY

VERLAINE *lets himself into the room. As before,* MATHILDE *lies naked, facedown on the bed.*

VERLAINE *turns to close the door behind him. When he turns back,* MATHILDE *has vanished.*

> RIMBAUD (V.O.)
> Have we lived together for two years to finish up like this?

INT. ROOM IN THE HÔTEL LIEGÈOIS NIGHT

VERLAINE *sits, motionless,* RIMBAUD's *letter in his hand, tears running down his cheeks.*

RIMBAUD (V.O.)

Think back to what you were before you met me. Listen to your heart. I'm yours for always.

VERLAINE *crumples up the letter and throws it across the room.*

EXT. DOCKS AT ANTWERP DAY

RIMBAUD, *carrying a battered cardboard suitcase, comes down the gangplank of the London ferry, on to Antwerp docks.*

INT. ROOM IN THE HÔTEL DE COURTRAI NIGHT

The same shabby room VERLAINE *and* RIMBAUD *occupied the year before. Now, the two of them are locked in a violent struggle, swaying in a grim embrace, wrestling and throwing punches, until* RIMBAUD *is lying on top of* VERLAINE, *pinning him to the ground. Stalemate: and eventually* RIMBAUD *rolls off* VERLAINE, *sighs and passes a hand in front of his eyes.*

RIMBAUD

I'll go back to Paris tomorrow.

VERLAINE

No, look, it won't happen again, I'll never walk out on you again, I promise.

RIMBAUD

No, you won't. I'm not giving you the chance. What was I supposed to do in London with no money?

VERLAINE

I'm sorry, I was very hurt.

RIMBAUD

Why? God knows, I've said far worse things to you than that. And you really did look a cunt.

VERLAINE, *who's on his feet again, looks as if he's on the verge of flaring up: then he controls himself and slumps into a chair.*

Dissolve.

Later: VERLAINE *sits in the same position, in the dark, watching* RIMBAUD, *who lies asleep in the double bed.*

Dissolve.

INT.   ROOM IN THE HÔTEL DE COURTRAI   DAWN

The next morning, very early: RIMBAUD *wakes to find himself, rather to his surprise, alone in the room.*

EXT.   PASSAGE SAINT-HUBERT, BRUSSELS   DAY

It's still early, but already a blazing hot day. VERLAINE*'s nevertheless wearing a heavy overcoat. He stands in the doorway of a small shop, peering in the window, swaying slightly, his eyes already bleary with drink.*

INT.   ROOM IN THE HÔTEL DE COURTRAI   DAY

It's noon now on a sweltering hot day. The windows are wide open, to no particular effect, the net curtains hanging limp in the absence of a breath of air. RIMBAUD, *his expression melancholy and exhausted, moves slowly round the room, gathering up his effects and stuffing them in his decrepit suitcase. The door suddenly bursts open to admit* VERLAINE, *plainly in a state of over-excitement.*

> RIMBAUD

Where have you been?

> VERLAINE

Out. I went, I went to the Spanish Embassy again, to see if they would change their minds. But they wouldn't, it's ridiculous, it's fucking ridiculous. I'm willing to fight, I said, and die for your cause, you can't afford to turn away volunteers. But they said they weren't taking on any foreigners. Then, I said, you deserve to lose the fucking war and I hope you do.

> RIMBAUD

And were you at the Spanish Embassy all morning?

VERLAINE

No.

RIMBAUD

You're drunk.

VERLAINE

I have yes had a few drinks.

He suddenly notices what RIMBAUD *is doing.*

What are you doing?

RIMBAUD

Packing.

VERLAINE

Where are you going?

RIMBAUD

I'm going back home to Roche, I'm going to finish my book
and I'm going to have it published.

VERLAINE

Oh, published? I thought you were far too important for that.

RIMBAUD *doesn't answer, refusing to rise to the bait.*

Anyway, listen, we're going back to London.

RIMBAUD

We are not going back to London.

VERLAINE

Yes, look, I've been thinking it over, it's by far the best idea.

RIMBAUD

Then why did you go to the Spanish Embassy?

VERLAINE

I didn't.

Silence. RIMBAUD *pushes some more clothes into his suitcase.*

Don't go. Think it over.

RIMBAUD

I've thought it over.

VERLAINE *paces for a moment. He seems increasingly agitated.*

VERLAINE

Do you realise what day it is tomorrow?

RIMBAUD

Friday.

VERLAINE

It's my wedding anniversary. And I haven't seen her, my wife, since we made love here, in Brussels, nearly a year ago. She won't answer my letters. Do you know, I wrote to her last week and told her if she didn't come to Brussels within three days, I'd commit suicide? And she didn't even answer.

RIMBAUD

Ah, but then you didn't commit suicide.

VERLAINE

I suppose you think that's funny.

RIMBAUD

No, it's pitiful. How many people did you write and tell you were going to commit suicide? I'm surprised you didn't send out invitations.

VERLAINE

How can you be so callous?

RIMBAUD

Callous? You abandon me in London and then summon me to Brussels and expect me to hang around while you decide whether you're going to go back to your wife, join the army or shoot yourself. Then, when you fail to achieve any of these aims, as you undoubtedly will, you want me to go back to London with you. I'm not going to. It's all over. I'm leaving you.

VERLAINE

You can't. You can't.

VERLAINE *stops pacing. He takes* RIMBAUD *by the arm, trying to engage his attention and distract him from his packing.*

Look, it's summer. Don't you remember last summer, when we set out, how wonderful it was? I remember evenings . . . Why don't we go south? Late summer on the Mediterranean, we could dedicate ourselves to warmth. Or Africa, I know you've always wanted to go to Africa. Just for a month and then make up your mind. Look at the sun.

EXT. ABYSSINIAN PLATEAU DAY

The sun-baked plains far below and the distant sea.

INT. ROOM IN THE HÔTEL DE COURTRAI DAY

RIMBAUD *opens his eyes, maintains the silence a little longer.*

                    RIMBAUD
No.

                    VERLAINE
Why not?

RIMBAUD *looks at* VERLAINE, *his expression serene, his voice gentle.*

                    RIMBAUD
I can't. It's no good. It's too late.

                    VERLAINE
It's not. I promise you it's not. You know if you leave me, you'll kill me. I can't bear to be alone. I don't exist without someone else. I don't care if you stay with me out of pity, as long as you stay.

                    RIMBAUD
I can't.

                    VERLAINE
Why not? Don't you care? Have you no idea what this means to me?

87

RIMBAUD

Oh, for God's sake, stop whining.

VERLAINE *goes over to look out of the window. He mops at his brow with a greyish handkerchief.*

VERLAINE

It's very hot.

RIMBAUD

Take your coat off.

VERLAINE

I will.

He slips his coat off, walks over to the door and hangs it up.

I did some shopping this morning.

He fumbles in the pocket of his coat, finally getting hold of something.

I bought a gun.

He points the revolver at RIMBAUD, *who looks at him, perfectly unmoved.*

RIMBAUD

What for?

VERLAINE

For you. And for me. For everybody.

RIMBAUD

I hope you bought plenty of ammunition.

VERLAINE *reaches for a chair and puts it in front of the door; then he sits astride it, pointing the revolver over the back of it at* RIMBAUD. RIMBAUD *leans against the far wall, grinning.*

VERLAINE

I'm not going to let you go, you know.

RIMBAUD

Well, this is rather an entertaining number. We haven't seen this one before.

VERLAINE

I'll kill you!

RIMBAUD

Oh, pull yourself together.

VERLAINE

I read your letter. You begged me to come back. You said you were crying as you wrote. I could see your tears on the paper!

RIMBAUD

Well, that was before I thought of pawning your clothes.

VERLAINE *springs to his feet, shaking with rage. He raises the revolver and fires at* RIMBAUD, *then, apparently stunned by the noise of the report, fires again into the floor.* RIMBAUD, *meanwhile, is clutching at his left wrist, staring at it in amazement and horror, as the blood pours down over his hand. He shies away, as* VERLAINE *moves towards him.*

VERLAINE

Oh, God, I'm sorry, I didn't mean to.

RIMBAUD

Look what you've done.

VERLAINE

I'm sorry, I didn't mean to.

RIMBAUD

Look.

VERLAINE *bursts into tears. He tries to give* RIMBAUD *the revolver.*

VERLAINE

Oh, for God's sake, kill me, kill me, shoot me.

RIMBAUD

What?

VERLAINE

Shoot me.

RIMBAUD

How can I, you silly bugger, you've just blown a hole in my hand.

89

VERLAINE *drops the revolver as if his fingers were burnt;* RIMBAUD
begins to laugh hysterically.

> VERLAINE

Oh, God, what have I done?

> RIMBAUD

You missed.

EXT. PLACE ROUPPE EVENING

RIMBAUD's *arm is bandaged and in a sling. He and* VERLAINE, *who's
still wearing his heavy overcoat, are crossing the square on their way to
the station.* RIMBAUD *carries his old suitcase in his good hand. A few
paces in silence, then* VERLAINE *turns to* RIMBAUD, *his face working.*

> VERLAINE

What can I say to make you stay?

RIMBAUD *completely ignores him. Something seems to snap in*
VERLAINE. *All of a sudden, he hurries a few paces ahead, turns and
begins to fumble in his pocket.*

All right, watch this!

After a second's hesitation, RIMBAUD *turns and makes a run for it.*
VERLAINE *sets off in hot pursuit, struggling to free his revolver, which he
finally succeeds in doing.* RIMBAUD *ducks and weaves across the crowded
square, occasionally checking back over his shoulder to see if* VERLAINE *is
gaining on him. At a certain point, when he's doing this, he cannons
directly into a uniformed* POLICEMAN, *who is immediately aware that
something untoward is occurring and grabs* RIMBAUD *by his unban-
daged arm.*

> POLICEMAN

What's going on?

> RIMBAUD

He's trying to kill me!

The POLICEMAN *turns on* VERLAINE, *who skids to a halt and, after a
moment's reflection, starts trying to stuff his revolver back in his pocket.*

INT. COURTROOM IN BRUSSELS DAY

VERLAINE *stands humbly in the courtroom facing the magistrate,* JUDGE THEODORE T'SERSTEVENS, *a figure of icy severity.*

> JUDGE
> What exactly are you doing in Brussels?

> VERLAINE
> I was hoping my wife might come and join me here, as she had already done on one occasion since our separation.

> JUDGE
> I fail to see how the departure of a friend could have cast you into such despair. Did there perhaps exist between you and Rimbaud other relations besides those of friendship?

> VERLAINE
> No. This is a suggestion slanderously invented by my wife and her family.

The JUDGE *contemplates* VERLAINE *through narrowed eyes.*

INT. PRISON HOSPITAL DAY

VERLAINE *is escorted into the plain room, his expression apprehensive. There are two* DOCTORS *in the room, one of whom is putting on a pair of rubber gloves. The other indicates a kind of shelf running along one of the walls at waist-height.*

> DOCTOR
> Take all your clothes off and lie on this, face down.

INT. SURGERY IN SAINT-JEAN HOSPITAL DAY

CLOSE ON RIMBAUD, *his face contorted with pain. He gasps in sudden agony and there's the* SOUND *of a metallic clang.*

This turns out to be the bloodstained bullet, dropped from between the SURGEON'*s forceps into a kidney-bowl. He nods briskly to* RIMBAUD *to signify the ordeal is over.*

91

INT. COURTROOM DAY

The JUDGE *peers at* VERLAINE *over the top of his glasses.*

> JUDGE
>
> Both doctors have testified that on the basis of their examination they are satisfied that you have recently indulged in both active and passive sodomy.

> VERLAINE
>
> Have they?

> JUDGE
>
> So do you deny you are a practising sodomist?

> VERLAINE
>
> The word is sodomite.

> JUDGE
>
> Whatever the word may be, the activity it describes is not one which is encouraged in Brussels.

EXT. SAINT-JEAN HOSPITAL DAY

RIMBAUD *emerges from the hospital, his arm in a sling, carrying his cardboard suitcase. He stands for a moment, looking one way then another, blinking in the blazing sunlight.*

INT. COURTROOM DAY

VERLAINE *rises to his feet and stands facing the bench.* JUDGE T'SERSTEVENS *clears his throat.*

> JUDGE
>
> Paul-Marie Verlaine, the court finds you guilty under Article 399 of the Penal Code of grievous bodily harm and sentences you . . .

The JUDGE *glances at* VERLAINE, *his eyes suddenly sparkling with malice.*

> . . . to a fine of two hundred francs and two years' imprisonment.

VERLAINE *is staggered by the severity of the sentence; his mouth drops open in shock.*

EXT. COURTYARD OF THE RIMBAUD FARM AT ROCHE DAY

It is another blazing hot day. RIMBAUD, *carrying his case, his arm in a sling, shuffles across the dusty courtyard.*

INT. FARMHOUSE KITCHEN DAY

MME RIMBAUD, ISABELLE, VITALIE *and* FRÉDÉRIC *are all sitting at the table, eating lunch.* RIMBAUD's *chair is empty. They all look up as* RIMBAUD *opens the door and appears on the threshold, and variously react to his haggard, wild-eyed expression. It's his mother who finally speaks.*

> MME RIMBAUD
>
> Now what's the matter?

RIMBAUD *drops his suitcase and advances a couple of paces into the room.*

> RIMBAUD
>
> Verlaine.

He reaches his seat at the table and subsides onto it. ISABELLE *is watching him intently, as he speaks again.*

> Verlaine!

He puts his arms on the table and buries his face in them. His body is shaken with sobs. The others watch him in constrained silence.

INT. HAYLOFT DAY

RIMBAUD *sits at his makeshift desk, writing with his child's pen. After a moment he looks up and stares out into space, lost in thought.*

EXT. PRISON AT MONS DAY

VERLAINE, *in his blue canvas prison uniform, shuffles alongside the other prisoners as they exercise, moving in a slow, dispirited circle around the narrow confines of the prison yard.*

INT. HAYLOFT DAY

RIMBAUD *writes on, concentrating intently.*

EXT. ABYSSINIAN PLATEAU DAY

The jolting progress, the flap of white canvas.

INT. PRISON WORKSHOP DAY

VERLAINE *is one of a long row of prisoners painfully pushing needles through the coarse hemp of yet another mailbag.*

INT. HAYLOFT DAY

RIMBAUD *paces up and down, pen in hand.*

EXT. SEA DAY

The sun beats down on the surface of a glassy sea.

INT. PRISON CELL NIGHT

VERLAINE *sits alone in his cell, indirectly lit, motionless except for his right hand, which slowly tells the beads of his rosary.*

INT. HAYLOFT NIGHT

RIMBAUD *works on by candlelight, crouched over his desk.*

EXT. DECK OF A DHOW DAY

The sea again, seen from a prone position on the deck, with the elegant curve of the dhow's sail cutting into the margin of the image.

EXT. COURTYARD AT ROCHE DAY

ISABELLE *stops in her tracks: what's stopped her is a terrible animal howling from the loft above the barn.*

INT. KITCHEN NIGHT

A candle casts a pool of light across the wooden table as MME RIMBAUD, *her back straight as a rod, turns the final page of* RIMBAUD*'s manuscript and finishes reading.* RIMBAUD, *his eyes feverishly bright, watches her from an armchair near the door.* ISABELLE *also sits in a corner, but she is watching* RIMBAUD. MME RIMBAUD *looks up from the manuscript.*

MME RIMBAUD

What does it mean? I don't understand what it's supposed to mean.

RIMBAUD

It means exactly what it says, word for word, no more, no less.

MME RIMBAUD *looks at him, skeptical, unblinking.*

EXT. COURTYARD AT ROCHE DAY

A POSTMAN *trudges across the courtyard, carrying a parcel.* RIMBAUD *bursts out of the house and intercepts him, snatching the parcel from him.*

Over this, the voice of the adult ISABELLE.

ISABELLE (V.O.)

My mother paid for his book to be published, you know. . . .

INT. HAYLOFT DAY

RIMBAUD *impatiently rips the parcel open and takes out one of several copies of a slim pamphlet-sized volume of not much more than fifty pages, the title in red on a buff cover, the title-page arranged as follows:*

A. RIMBAUD

UNE

SAISON EN ENFER

PRIX: UN FRANC

He reaches for his old knife and begins to cut the pages.

ISABELLE (V.O.)

. . . and even though, as far as I know, it only sold six copies . . .

*He cuts the pages with increasing eagerness and, as it's a slim volume,
he's soon finished; then he opens the book at random and begins to read.
It takes only a few seconds for the excitement to vanish; clearly it's
replaced by a wave of cruel disillusionment. He extends his arm, disgust
in his eyes, and lets the book drop onto the floor.*

EXT. FARMHOUSE AT ROCHE DAY

RIMBAUD *alone, no luggage, strides away from the farm.* ISABELLE
stands in the doorway, watching him leave.

ISABELLE (V.O.)

. . . that should prove to you we're not opposed to his work
becoming known.

INT. ANDRÉ'S EVENING 1892

VERLAINE *shifts uncomfortably; he can't quite see where the conversation
is leading and it's making him uneasy.*

VERLAINE

No, of course not.

ISABELLE

All the same, my mother and I are determined to get hold of
all his writings.

VERLAINE

I don't quite . . .

ISABELLE

The point is, Monsieur Verlaine, to speak frankly, a number of
the poems he wrote in extreme youth were quite . . . indecent
and, in some cases, even profane. He would never have wished
to be remembered for them.

VERLAINE

So . . .

ISABELLE

Yes: my mother and I plan to, as it were, separate the wheat

96

from the tares and destroy those of his works we feel he would
have destroyed himself.

Silence. VERLAINE *is appalled.*

> VERLAINE

I see.

> ISABELLE

What you may not know is that Arthur was converted.

> VERLAINE

Converted?

> ISABELLE

I reasoned with him and prayed for him for weeks while he was
ill, and eventually he asked to be confessed. God kept him alive
long enough to repent, so that he could be saved.

VERLAINE *is moved. He sips at his absinthe, then looks up at* ISABELLE.

> VERLAINE

The last time we met we spoke of religion. I hadn't seen him
for a couple of years: I'd been away . . . staying at a monastery
in Belgium; and he had that teaching job in Germany. I tried
very hard to convince him of the truth . . .

He breaks off. ISABELLE *is looking at him, her expression skeptical.*

EXT. BLACK FOREST NIGHT 1875

*A clearing in a pine forest close to Stuttgart on the bank of a narrow
tributary of the Neckar. There's a full moon in a cloudless sky, snow on
the ground and thin ice on the edges of the river.* RIMBAUD *appears, a
little better dressed than is usual;* VERLAINE, *swathed in a capacious
Inverness cape, follows a few paces behind. Their breath rises on the
frosty air; both are a little the worse for drink.*

> VERLAINE

You must understand, I've changed completely. All I want now
is to lead a quiet, simple life with God. It happened quite suddenly, the day the governor told me Mathilde had been
granted her divorce. I lay down and looked at my life and there

was nothing, nothing. It seemed to me the only thing I could do was to submit myself to God and ask Him to forgive me and help me face my situation. And He did. I promise you, He did.

RIMBAUD

And now you want us to love each other in Jesus, am I right?

VERLAINE

I want you to follow my example.

RIMBAUD *stops in the clearing and utters a harsh bark of laughter.* VERLAINE *puts a hand on his arm.*

I hope you didn't think, all this time, I might be angry with you.

RIMBAUD

No.

VERLAINE

I know you had no idea I might be put away for so long; I certainly forgave you for it.

RIMBAUD

I didn't forgive you.

VERLAINE

What for?

RIMBAUD

For missing.

VERLAINE *laughs uneasily, but* RIMBAUD *doesn't appear to be joking. He's looking out across the river now;* VERLAINE *watches him uncertainly for a moment, then shivers suddenly.*

VERLAINE

Not very warm, is it?

RIMBAUD

Why did you come here?

VERLAINE *is taken aback by the hostility of his tone.*

VERLAINE

Well . . . because I want you to find some direction in your life.
I want God to help you achieve your aims.

RIMBAUD

Aims? I have no aims.

VERLAINE

I mean your writing.

RIMBAUD

I've stopped writing.

VERLAINE

I don't understand. . . .

RIMBAUD

Then let me put it another way: I no longer write.

VERLAINE

Why not?

RIMBAUD

Because I have nothing more to say. If I ever had anything to say in the first place.

VERLAINE *gapes at him, completely bewildered.*

I used to have some idea that what I did would make a difference, you know, change the world. I thought nothing would ever be the same again. But it's no good, the world is too old, there's nothing new, it's all been said.

VERLAINE

Not in the way you can say it. You have a gift. It's no good throwing it away because your expectations were unrealistic. It's the expectations you should change.

RIMBAUD

It's my gift, I can do what I like with it.

VERLAINE

But . . . what else is there?

RIMBAUD

Anything that comes along. Anywhere away out of this mortuary: Europe. You can't change corpses, they have their own rhythms. So, somewhere *newer.*

VERLAINE

You can't give up, you've hardly begun.

RIMBAUD

Don't worry, I'll be very good at it, no one will be able to touch me: the master of silence.

VERLAINE

If we don't, who's going to tell the truth?

RIMBAUD

Three years ago, you said the truth was this and the truth was that. Then along comes an angel of the Lord and the next day the truth is something completely different.

VERLAINE

But I've changed: change, I thought that was what you wanted.

100

RIMBAUD
You've changed, have you?

VERLAINE
Yes!

Silence. Eventually RIMBAUD *turns to face him.*

RIMBAUD
Then here, in the wilderness, I offer you an archetypal choice:
the choice between my body and my soul.

CLOSE *on* VERLAINE: *he's caught in an agonising dilemma.*

RIMBAUD (V.O.)
Choose.

VERLAINE
Your body.

He's spoken very quietly: and RIMBAUD's *response is a wintry, contemptuous smile.*

RIMBAUD
See, the ninety-eight wounds of Our Saviour burst and bleed.

VERLAINE *stretches out a hand to touch his cheek.*

Don't.

VERLAINE
Aren't my sins a matter for my own conscience?

RIMBAUD
They would be if you had one.

VERLAINE
Why should it matter to you?

RIMBAUD
Because I hate your miserable weakness.

VERLAINE
I see no clash between loving God and loving you.

RIMBAUD
Come on, let's go back.

He starts to move off, but VERLAINE *catches at his sleeve.*

VERLAINE
No, listen, I sat in my cell and thought how happy we could be, it should be easy, it should be the easiest thing in the world, why isn't it?

RIMBAUD
It never worked for us. And it will never work for either of us.

VERLAINE
I wanted us to go away together.

RIMBAUD
Yes.

VERLAINE
What am I going to do?

RIMBAUD
You'll have to go and find somebody else.

VERLAINE
I can't. Please.

He puts his arms round RIMBAUD, *pinioning him.*

Please.

RIMBAUD
Let me go.

VERLAINE *clings onto him:* RIMBAUD *speaks, as he has throughout this last exchange, with great weariness.*

Let go.

VERLAINE
Please.

RIMBAUD *wrenches free one of his arms and hits* VERLAINE *in the face, stunning him. Then he hits him again, hard, several times, methodically, until he collapses in an untidy heap, sprawled out across the cracking ice.* RIMBAUD *hauls him back onto the bank and kneels beside him, straightening out his body in an oddly tender way.*

102

EXT. RIVERBANK DAY 1870

RIMBAUD *kneels, holding the hand of the dead Prussian soldier.*

EXT. BLACK FOREST NIGHT 1875

RIMBAUD, *on his knees, props* VERLAINE *against a tree. Blood from* VERLAINE*'s nose makes black streaks on the snow. When he's arranged the body,* RIMBAUD *waits awhile, looking down at his unconscious friend. Then he leans forward and kisses him on the top of his high fore-head, and rises to his feet.*

RIMBAUD

Goodbye.

He turns and walks away, leaves the clearing, not looking back.

EXT. MAIN SQUARE IN HARAR, ABYSSINIA DAY 1883

An abrupt CUT; *and* RIMBAUD *is still walking away from the* CAMERA, *across the deserted square, towards the fiery ball of the morning sun. Strange, percussive* MUSIC *which, as he turns a corner, proves to be ema-nating from a spectacular procession. Everyone, man and woman, is in dazzling white robes, with the exception of the priest and his retinue, who wear rich regalia, heavy with gold thread, and are sheltered under exquisite azure parasols with gold fringing carried by acolytes. The* MUSICIANS *play large flutes, bells, heavy drums. The entire procession turns into the Coptic cathedral, ready for the Christmas mass.*

RIMBAUD *pauses for the merest instant, then moves on, against the flow of the procession, heading away from the cathedral. He's twenty-eight now, lean and tanned, his cropped hair already flecked with grey.*

Over this, a caption:

VI   L'ECLAIR

EXT. ABYSSINIAN PLATEAU DAY

RIMBAUD *strides, at punishing speed, across a savage, rocky terrain. The* CAMERA *pulls slowly up and away to reveal his isolation in the immense, empty, pitiless landscape.*

103

EXT. MARKETPLACE IN HARAR DAY

RIMBAUD *walks through the bustling marketplace, crowded with women in dazzlingly colourful robes. He's the only white man in the crowd and seems, moving purposefully through the hubbub, even more isolated than in the previous scene.*

EXT. COURTYARD OF THE TRADING POST AT HARAR DAY

The trading post run by RIMBAUD *is a modest general store, the business of which spills out into a dusty courtyard.* RIMBAUD *moves across the courtyard, nodding brusquely to one or two of his assistants, who are engaged in various transactions in and around the entrance to the store.* RIMBAUD'*s destination, however, is not the store, but an extraordinary dark wooden house, towering over one end of the courtyard, its style a kind of Indian Gothic, its windows glazed with panes stained different primary colours in an apparently random design.* RIMBAUD *disappears into the house.*

INT. RIMBAUD'S HOUSE IN HARAR DAY

RIMBAUD'*s houseboy,* DJAMI, *a boy of about fifteen, kneels to pull off* RIMBAUD'*s high leather boots. A handsome young* SOMALIAN WOMAN *brings him a bowl of cool water.*

INT. DINING-ROOM IN RIMBAUD'S HOUSE EVENING

RIMBAUD *sits at the plain table: the* SOMALIAN WOMAN *serves him a meal: some kind of meat and lentil stew with unleavened bread.*

INT. BEDROOM IN RIMBAUD'S HOUSE NIGHT

A large room, empty except for the single bed in the corner, strangely lit by the moon shining through the panes of stained glass. RIMBAUD *makes love to the* SOMALIAN WOMAN, *dim shapes, white on black.*

EXT. COURTYARD OF THE TRADING POST DAY

RIMBAUD *has set up a heavy camera on a tripod in the centre of the courtyard. He finishes instructing a giggling* DJAMI *and makes his way*

to the entrance of the trading post, a dark breach in the crumbling stone
wall. He rests a hand on the doorjamb, signals, and DJAMI presses the
button, startled by the mild explosion of the magnesium flare.

INT. ANDRÉ'S EVENING 1892

CLOSE on VERLAINE's hand, as it moves among a number of black
and white photographs of RIMBAUD, mostly awkwardly posed, sometimes in Harar, sometimes against tropical vegetation, in the later ones
wearing a vestigial moustache, his features ever more taut and skull-
like.

> VERLAINE
> Of course, it's seventeen years since I last saw him: but I
> wouldn't have recognised him from these. All that time, we
> heard nothing, except that he was travelling.

> ISABELLE
> Oh yes, he travelled a great deal: Aden, Alexandria, Batavia,
> Cyprus . . .

> VERLAINE
> Batavia.

EXT. PLAINS OF THE OGADEN DAY 1883

CLOSE on RIMBAUD: he's on horseback, riding fast, wearing a loose cotton shirt and canvas trousers.

> ISABELLE (V.O.)
> And Abyssinia. He opened a trading post there about ten years
> ago.

RIMBAUD'S P.O.V.: he's coming down onto a vast stretch of savannah,
dotted with gum trees and mimosa. In front of him, moving with exag-
gerated care through the long grass, are dozens of ostriches.

He explored the whole country. Places no white man had ever
been. He rode across the Ogaden.

RIMBAUD rides through the ostriches, which scatter indignantly in front
of his horse. He smiles to himself as the high grass parts before him.

EXT. ABYSSINIAN PLATEAU DAWN 1891

It's almost dawn and RIMBAUD *wakes on his bedroll by the ashes of his fire. He springs to his feet. Not far off is the edge of the plateau.* RIMBAUD *starts moving towards it, striding fast in his traditional fashion. He wants to reach the edge of the precipice in time to see the sunrise.*

Suddenly, he gasps in shock. He's caught his knee on a broken branch jaggedly protruding from a dead-looking thornbush.

He strides on and soon reaches the sheer drop at the edge of the plateau. Below, revealed, is the sea, and, as he watches, the disc of the sun slowly begins to appear.

RIMBAUD *looks down at his leg: through the slashed canvas of his trousers blood is beginning to well.*

He looks out across the sea again. As he stares at the sun, ISABELLE*'s voice again.*

> ISABELLE (V.O.)
> About a year ago, his trouble started.

> VERLAINE (V.O.)
> What was the matter with him?

> ISABELLE (V.O.)
> He had a tumour on his knee.

INT. ANDRÉ'S EVENING 1892

VERLAINE*'s head jerks up: he looks shocked.*

> VERLAINE
> That's very strange.

ISABELLE *pauses in the act of gathering up the photographs.*

> ISABELLE
> Why?

> VERLAINE
> Because that's what I have: a tumour on my knee.

106

INT. TRADING POST AT HARAR 1891

RIMBAUD, *his face pinched and haggard, lies on a couch installed in his store, between the counter and the window. His right leg, the knee visibly swollen, is stretched out on the couch; the left foot is planted on the floor. He's watching the comings and goings out in the yard, where one of his assistants pours coffee beans into a sack standing on a weighing machine.*

> ISABELLE (V.O.)
> It would have been all right if he'd done something about it, if he hadn't been so conscientious about his work. There was no doctor in Harar, but he insisted on staying until the pain became unbearable.

RIMBAUD *moves to catch one of his assistants' attention, then grimaces in agony.*

INT. ANDRÉ'S EVENING 1892

VERLAINE's *hand shakes a little as he pours water into his next absinthe.*

> ISABELLE
> He couldn't ride any more, so he designed himself a litter.

INT. RIMBAUD'S HOUSE AT HARAR 1891

RIMBAUD *has had a daybed set up in an upstairs room, by an open window with red and yellow panes. He hands out neat drawings of the skeleton of a tented litter to his Abyssinian assistants. In the background the* SOMALIAN WOMAN *looks on anxiously.*

> ISABELLE (V.O.)
> Then he hired sixteen men to carry him to the coast.

EXT. COURTYARD AT HARAR DAY

Several of RIMBAUD's *assistants work with wooden battens and canvas sheets: atmosphere of intense concentration.*

INT./EXT. RIMBAUD'S HOUSE DAY

RIMBAUD, *black circles of pain below his eyes, watches intently.*

HIS P.O.V.: *down in the yard, the litter is taking shape.*

RIMBAUD *watches, his eyes burning.*

EXT. COURTYARD DAY

The courtyard, for once, is quite deserted. Only the litter, seen from above, ramshackle and bizarre under its canvas roof, stands in hyper-real isolation, as if it has just landed from space.

INT. ANDRÉ'S EVENING 1892

ISABELLE *closes her eyes briefly, as painful memories crowd in.*

> ISABELLE
> The journey took more than two weeks.

VERLAINE *thinks about this, glass in hand.*

INT. RIMBAUD'S HOUSE DAY 1891

DJAMI *and two other servants lift* RIMBAUD *from his daybed: he cries out. They carry him, as gently as they can, out of the room.*

In the background, watching, is the SOMALIAN WOMAN: *but she doesn't accompany them. Instead, she moves over to the daybed, lies down on it and turns her face to the wall.*

EXT. COURTYARD DAY

It's raining. DJAMI *and the servants lower* RIMBAUD *into the litter. He cries out again, clearly in terrible pain.* DJAMI *leans across and kisses his forehead. The sixteen* BEARERS, *all in white, take up their positions and the litter is raised. From within it, another groan of unbearable agony.*

EXT. OUTSKIRTS OF HARAR DAY

The BEARERS *move as fast as they can, slipping and sliding on the wet red earth as they carry the litter down a steep slope. It's still raining. Behind the litter is a small procession: a few camels, carrying supplies for the expedition. Now, the litter lurches horribly as one of the* BEARERS *slips, and* RIMBAUD *cries out in anguish.*

EXT. ABYSSINIAN PLATEAU EVENING

An appalling storm is in progress. The BEARERS *have taken what shelter they can under a huge eucalyptus. The litter stands, out on its own, in the torrential rain, buffeted by a howling wind.*

CLOSE *on* RIMBAUD: *the canvas is completely ineffectual shelter and the slanting rain lashes down on* RIMBAUD.

> VERLAINE (V.O.)
> He was always searching for a solution, a place, a formula. Do you think he ever found them?

A flash of jagged lightning and a tremendous thunderclap.

> ISABELLE (V.O.)
> Oh, yes.

RIMBAUD's *face is screwed up with pain and misery: it's impossible to tell if it's rainwater or tears coursing down his cheeks.*

EXT. ABYSSINIAN PLATEAU DAY

As in RIMBAUD's *dream, the jolting movement, the canvas flapping* IN *and* OUT OF SHOT.

> ISABELLE (V.O.)
> Yes, I know he did.

EXT. ABYSSINIAN PLATEAU DAY

The astonishing view of rock face and coastal strip and silver sea: the landscape is violent and unforgiving, but of an unearthly beauty.

CLOSE *on* RIMBAUD, *as he looks out and down at the vista spread before him. Finally he turns his head and speaks.*

> RIMBAUD

On. On!

His face starts to sway and pucker with pain as the BEARERS *raise the litter and move on.*

Fade.

EXT. SEA DAY

The sun beats down on the surface of the sea.

Over this, a caption:

> VII   MATIN

EXT. DECK OF A DHOW DAY

As before, the sea seen from the deck, part of the dhow's sail curving down the edge of FRAME.

ANOTHER ANGLE *reveals* RIMBAUD, *who lies on a stained, filthy, thin mattress on the deck, inadequately shaded from the pitiless sun. Pain has wasted him, he looks ethereal, transparent.*

> VERLAINE (V.O.)

I shall return with limbs of steel, a dark skin and a wrathful eye. I shall have money: I shall be cruel and idle. I'll be saved.

INT. ANDRÉ'S EVENING 1892

ISABELLE *is looking across at* VERLAINE, *uncertainly.*

> ISABELLE

What?

> VERLAINE

Something he wrote.

ISABELLE *frowns, evidently unfamiliar with the passage.*

110

ISABELLE
Well, of course, he *was* saved. But not right away.

INT. OPERATING THEATER AT THE HOSPITAL OF THE IMMACU-
LATE CONCEPTION IN MARSEILLES DAY 1891

CLOSE *on the harsh, set mould of* MME RIMBAUD *'s features.*

ISABELLE (V.O.)
First, as soon as he arrived, he went into hospital in Marseilles.

A WIDER ANGLE *shows most of the plain white room.* MME RIMBAUD, *in her invariable black, stands against one of the walls.* RIMBAUD *is stretched out on the operating table, his bare right leg disfigured by an enormous, discoloured swelling, his head propped up on a bolster, his hands outstretched and secured in linen slings. The* SURGEON, *who is wearing a kind of butcher's apron, finishes rolling up his sleeves and picks up an instrument like a fine-toothed hacksaw.*

And they cut off his leg.

RIMBAUD *'s hand flutters, opens, reaches out towards his mother.*

MME RIMBAUD *sees, but does not respond. She stays where she is, her expression stony.*

The SURGEON *arrives, saw in hand, rests his other hand for a moment lightly on* RIMBAUD *'s thigh, fearsomely high up. He nods to his* ASSIS-TANT, *who steps forward, pours some chloroform onto a wad of cotton and lays it across* RIMBAUD *'s mouth and nose.*

RIMBAUD *'s eyes, which have still not left his mother, glaze and close.*

Blackout.

EXT. COURTYARD AT ROCHE DAY

ISABELLE *hurries across the courtyard. Once again, a terrible howl of anguish, this time from the main house rather than the barn.* ISABELLE *breaks into a run, disappearing into the house. It's a dark, cloudy day, rain in the air.*

111

INT. RIMBAUD'S BEDROOM DAY

RIMBAUD *lies on a single bed in a small, pleasant, simply furnished room. There's a vase of flowers on the bedside table.* RIMBAUD *is shivering, his face is running with sweat.* ISABELLE *hurries into the room and over to him.*

ISABELLE

What's the matter?

RIMBAUD

Can you see those carriages, driving across the sky?

He's pointing to the window. ISABELLE *takes his hand and sits next to the bed.*

I have to help others, you see: it's my duty.

ISABELLE

I know you do.

She starts to sponge his face with a damp flannel. He says something to her in Arabic, then repeats it, his expression agitated.

RIMBAUD

I don't want money, unless it's drenched in blood.

ISABELLE

Ssh.

RIMBAUD

Maybe the sea can wash away the stains.

ISABELLE

Maybe.

RIMBAUD

There's one thing, Isabelle, you must promise me; it's very important, will you promise?

ISABELLE

What?

RIMBAUD *points to the corner of the room, where an artificial leg is propped.*

RIMBAUD
Never let them amputate.

EXT. COUNTRY LANE NEAR ROCHE DAY

It's overcast and blustery. RIMBAUD, *manoeuvering heavy crutches and wearing his wooden leg, moves unsteadily, laboriously down the straight road. At every step he winces with effort, his progress agonisingly slow.*

INT. RIMBAUD'S BEDROOM DAY

ISABELLE *helps* RIMBAUD *off with his shirt; he grunts with pain, as the shirt comes off to reveal pulpy red wounds in his armpits caused by the wooden crutches.*

INT. ISABELLE'S BEDROOM NIGHT

ISABELLE *starts awake at the* SOUND *of a heavy crash and cry of pain from* RIMBAUD. *She scrambles out of bed, fumbling for the bedside oil-lamp.*

INT. RIMBAUD'S BEDROOM NIGHT

ISABELLE *lets herself into the room and her lamp reveals a horrifying image:* RIMBAUD, *one-legged, naked, lies face down on the carpet.* ISABELLE *drops to her knees beside him.*

RIMBAUD
It's time to go.

ISABELLE
What do you mean?

RIMBAUD
It's dawn. The caravan is leaving for the coast: the ivory, the musk. Saddle my horse.

ISABELLE
You're dreaming, it's the middle of the night.

RIMBAUD *looks up at her, his blue eyes wide open and lucid.*

RIMBAUD

No. No, it's the morning.

Fade.

EXT. FARMHOUSE AT ROCHE DAY

A storm is raging. The rain is blown almost horizontal by violent gusts of wind. A crash of thunder.

Over this, a caption:

VIII   ADIEU

INT. ANDRÉ'S EVENING 1892

CLOSE *on* ISABELLE, *as she speaks, her voice soft and hypnotic.*

ISABELLE

The drugs they gave him for the pain made him delirious. So he refused to go on with them.

INT. RIMBAUD'S BEDROOM DAY

RIMBAUD *groans with pain as he shifts his position slightly.* ISABELLE *sits beside him, feeding him soup. Outside, the storm continues.*

RIMBAUD

Autumn already. Time we were leaving. Let's leave. I need the sun.

INT. ANDRÉ'S EVENING 1892

ISABELLE *looks across the table at* VERLAINE.

ISABELLE

He would only stay at home a month. He kept saying he had to travel back towards the sun, that the sun would heal him . . .

She breaks off, suddenly aware of EUGÉNIE *looming over them.* VERLAINE *sits up with a start.*

114

VERLAINE
Ah, Eugénie, this is Mademoiselle Rimbaud. She's . . .

EUGÉNIE
I don't care who she is: all I'm saying, you don't come back tonight, you'll find your things in the street.

She moves off, abruptly. ISABELLE *watches her for a moment, clearly a little shaken.*

VERLAINE
Take no notice.

ISABELLE
I think perhaps it's time I was going, Monsieur Verlaine.

VERLAINE
No, wait. Please. Just a minute. Finish telling me about . . . your brother.

EXT. FARMHOUSE AT ROCHE DAWN 1891

A couple of FARMHANDS *lift* RIMBAUD *into the back of a cart, where he sits in a space between two battered suitcases.* ISABELLE *climbs up next to the* DRIVER. MME RIMBAUD *stands, motionless, in the doorway to the farmhouse. It's a gloomy dawn, autumnal drizzle and fog.*

ISABELLE (V.O.)
I don't think there's very much more to tell.

At a sign from RIMBAUD, *the* DRIVER *flicks his whip over the tired-looking horse, and the cart heaves into motion.* RIMBAUD *winces, controls himself, lifts a hand to wave good-bye to his mother.*

RIMBAUD'S P.O.V.: *a jolting, retreating view of* MME RIMBAUD. *She doesn't respond to his wave, but stands, perfectly still and expressionless, watching her disappearing son.*

He left.

INT. ANDRÉ'S EVENING 1892

VERLAINE *listens, hanging on every word.*

115

ISABELLE

We got as far as Marseilles; but by the time he arrived, he was
so ill, he had to go straight back into hospital. He'd lost the use
of his right arm, and soon a large tumour appeared on the
inside of his stump.

VERLAINE *closes his eyes, briefly, then opens them again.*

VERLAINE'S P.O.V.: EUGÉNIE *is leaving the bar on the arm of a portly,
middle-aged* MAN.

VERLAINE *turns his attention back to* ISABELLE.

INT. OPEN WARD AT THE HOSPITAL OF THE IMMACULATE CON-
CEPTION DAY 1891

RIMBAUD *lies in bed with* ISABELLE *sitting close by, taking dictation from
him. The incurables' ward is flooded with sunlight.* RIMBAUD*'s right arm
and hand are entirely swathed in a thick bandage. He's unshaven and
pale, his eyes glittering with fever. He murmurs inaudibly:* ISABELLE
leans in close to hear, her pen flying across the paper.

ISABELLE (V.O.)

On the last day, he dictated a letter to a steamship company,
booking a passage to Aden. He wanted the sun so much.

INT. ANDRÉ'S EVENING 1892

VERLAINE *stares into space. Eventually,* ISABELLE *breaks the silence.*

ISABELLE

You have my card, don't you?

VERLAINE

What? Oh, yes . . . yes, I do.

He fumbles in a waistcoat pocket and produces the card.

ISABELLE

Will you send the manuscripts to that address?

VERLAINE

Erm, of course.

116

ISABELLE

Please don't forget. And rest assured we shall make a very careful selection of what is to survive.

VERLAINE

You know, from the time he left, it's all just been one long footnote.

ISABELLE*'s reaction is a thin smile; she rises to her feet and* VERLAINE *begins, with some difficulty, to struggle up from the table.*

ISABELLE

Please don't get up.

VERLAINE

Won't you let me see you to your hotel?

ISABELLE

No, no. It was an honour to meet such a distinguished poet.

VERLAINE

A pleasure to meet you, mademoiselle.

ISABELLE

Goodbye.

She shakes hands formally, turns and resolutely sets off, leaving the bar. VERLAINE *subsides into his chair again.*

VERLAINE

Absinthe. Two.

If ANDRÉ *is surprised by this order, he doesn't show it. He brings two glasses, sets one in front of* VERLAINE, *the other opposite.* VERLAINE *starts to pour the water very slowly over the sugarlump.*

VERLAINE (V.O.)

Since he died, I see him every night. My great and radiant sin.

He looks up. Sitting opposite him at the table is RIMBAUD, *seventeen again, picking at the table with his knife.*

VERLAINE

Tell me if you love me.

RIMBAUD
You know I'm very fond of you. We've been very happy sometimes.

He takes a sip of his absinthe.

Do you love me?

VERLAINE
Yes.

RIMBAUD
Then put your hands on the table.

VERLAINE
What?

RIMBAUD
Put your hands on the table.

VERLAINE *does so.*

Palm upwards.

VERLAINE *turns his hands palm upwards.* RIMBAUD *looks at them for a moment; then he leans forward and kisses them. Finally, he looks up at* VERLAINE, *a faint smile on his face.*

CLOSE *on* VERLAINE: *he looks across the table, his eyes misty with tears.*

ANOTHER ANGLE: RIMBAUD *has disappeared and* VERLAINE *stares out into space.*

EXT. STREET IN THE QUARTIER LATIN NIGHT

VERLAINE *stumbles home, down a deserted street. It's very late and very cold; there's snow in the air.* VERLAINE*'s breath rises towards the night.*

VERLAINE (V.O.)
We were always happy. Always, I remember.

INT. STAIRWAY TO VERLAINE'S LODGINGS NIGHT

VERLAINE *drags himself up the dark, uncarpeted staircase, swaying from side to side, ricocheting off the walls.*

VERLAINE (V.O.)
He's not dead, he's trapped and living inside me.

INT. VERLAINE'S LODGINGS NIGHT

VERLAINE *lets himself in, fumbles for matches and lights a single candle on his desk.*

VERLAINE
Eugénie? Are you there?

No answer. And the candle, when he moves it across the room, reveals an empty bed. He puts the candle down beside the bed, drops to his knees with a sigh and begins to root around, looking for something under the bed.

VERLAINE (V.O.)
As long as I live, he has some kind of flickering and limited life. It's always the same words and the same gestures—the same images: I walk behind him across a steep, ploughed field; I sit, talking to him in a darkening room, until I can barely see his profile and his expressive hands: I lie in bed at dawn and watch him sleeping and see how nervously his hand brushes at his cheek.

During this, VERLAINE *has fetched out from under the bed a big folder. He carries this over to the desk, then goes back for the candle, which he puts on the desk, opens the folder and spreads out with his hand its contents: all* RIMBAUD's *manuscripts, poems, letters, drawings, prose. He contemplates all this for a moment, then turns his attention to* ISABELLE's *card, which he's fetched out of his pocket. By now, there's silence: and he carefully tears up the visiting card, scattering the pieces.*

VERLAINE
I remember him of an evening and he lives.

He smiles a little to himself and moves OUT OF FRAME, *back towards the bed.*

The desk, the manuscripts, the fragments of visiting card, flickering candlelight.

EXT. ABYSSINIAN PLATEAU DAWN

RIMBAUD *springs to his feet and begins to hurry towards the edge of the plateau. But this time the* CAMERA *outpaces him, soaring on ahead and finally over the edge, until it hovers above the dazzling sea.*

Over this, the voices of RIMBAUD *and* VERLAINE.

> RIMBAUD (V.O.)
>
> I've found it.

> VERLAINE (V.O.)
>
> What?

> RIMBAUD (V.O.)
>
> Eternity
> It's the sun mingled
> With the sea.

White out.